# Courage, Marshal Ney

Last Stand of the Bravest of the Brave

# James Mace

Electronic Edition Copyright © 2014 by James Mace

All rights reserved as permitted under the U.S. Copyright Act of 1976, no part of this publication may be reproduced, distributed, or transmitted in any form or by any means, or stored in a database or retrieval system, without the prior permission of the publisher.

The characters and events portrayed in this book are based on actual persons and events, but are used fictitiously.

Legionary Books
Meridian, Idaho 83642, USA
http://www.legionarybooks.net

First eBook Edition: 2014

Published in the United States of America

Cover Image: *Marshal Michel Ney, duc d'Elchingen, prince de la Moskova*, by François Gérard

*Death is nothing, but to live defeated and inglorious is to die daily.*
- Napoleon Bonaparte

# The Works of James Mace

**The Artorian Chronicles**
Soldier of Rome: The Legionary
Soldier of Rome: The Sacrovir Revolt
Soldier of Rome: Heir to Rebellion
Soldier of Rome: The Centurion
Soldier of Rome: Journey to Judea
Soldier of Rome: The Last Campaign

**Artorian Novellas**
Centurion Valens and the Empress of Death
Empire Betrayed: The Fall of Sejanus

**The Great Jewish Revolt**
Kingdom of the Damned: Rebellion in Judea
Kingdom of the Damned: Vespasian's Fury

**Napoleonic Works**
Forlorn Hope: The Storming of Badajoz
I Stood With Wellington
Courage, Marshal Ney

# Table of Contents

Preface
Chapter I: The New Headmaster
Chapter II: The Guard is Broken
Chapter III: End of a Dynasty
Chapter IV: Last Gasps of the Empire
Chapter V: The Betrayal of Friends
Chapter VI: The Marshal's Sword
Chapter VII: Who Shall Judge Him?
Chapter VIII: False Justice
Chapter IX: Condemned
Chapter X: Son of France
Chapter XI: Shadowy Stratagems
Chapter XII: The Pieces are Set
Chapter XIII: Checkmate
Chapter XIV: The Execution
Chapter XV: Where Liberty Has Arisen
Chapter XVI: Death is Just the Beginning
Chapter XVII: The Empty Casket
Chapter XVIII: A Return to the Past
Chapter XIX: A Bloody Escape
Chapter XX: Lady of France
Chapter XXI: The Safety of Ones Enemies
Chapter XXII: Fouche's Downfall
Chapter XXIII: In the Shadow of the Iron Duke
Chapter XXIV: On to Bordeaux!
Chapter XXV: Relics of a Life Long-Lived

## Preface

In June of 1815, Napoleon Bonaparte's attempts at reclaiming the French Empire are destroyed on the field of Waterloo. In the months to follow, the restored Bourbon monarchy seeks retribution against many of the now-exiled emperor's former generals. Foremost, they demand that Michel Ney, Marshal of France, who had been called by both enemy and friend as 'The Bravest of the Brave', pay with his life.

In December, Ney is tried by the Chamber of Peers, convicted, and sentenced to death, in direct violation of the Treaty of Paris, which formally ended the Napoleonic Wars. In a strange twist of fate, Ney finds the unlikeliest of allies in his former nemesis, British Field Marshal Sir Arthur Wellesley, the Duke of Wellington. Just before dawn on 7 December 1815, with Marshal Ney waiting to be taken away to his execution, the Duke cryptically tells him, "Death is just the beginning."

Three years later, a quiet and mysterious stranger arrives in Cheraw, South Carolina to take up the position as headmaster of a local school. Loved by both his students and the community, a series of intriguing events will only add to the legends surrounding the enigmatic schoolteacher, who is clearly more than he appears.

# Chapter I: The New Headmaster

Cheraw, South Carolina
15 January, 1819
\*\*\*

The wind blew coldest during the hour before the sun rose. A single lantern lit the ground as the lone man wrapped in a greatcoat walked the narrow street in the hour before the sun rose. A farming community named after a local Native American tribe, the town of Cheraw, South Carolina, consisted of a single main street with a rather ornate town hall, a few shops, and a schoolhouse. It was to this last building the man with the lamp was walking.

His name was Colonel Benjamin Rogers. A wealthy cotton planter who had earned his commission during the War of 1812, he was also a respected magistrate within the township. The town of Cheraw had less than a thousand total residents and, as such, a man of Rogers' military status placed him in high regard within the small community. Though no longer on active service, he still held the colonelcy of local militia, and as a matter of respect was usually addressed by his rank.

His purpose this morning was to interview a man from Philadelphia, who had written to him asking if the position of headmaster for the local school was still vacant. Most of the plantation owners, along with all other families of prominence, were so desperate to find someone to teach their sons that they would have settled for anyone who could read and write. However, Rogers was determined to vet this stranger from up north thoroughly.

The colonel unlocked the double-doors of the schoolhouse and made his way past the vacant desks that were slowly gathering dust. He walked with a slight limp, a constant reminder of his more harrowing days, when he'd taken part in the ill-fated invasion of Canada during the last war with Britain. He opened the door to the headmaster's office with a loud creak, removing some old papers from the desk and making certain everything was tidy and in order. Just as he sat behind the small oak desk, he heard a knocking on the outer doors, which echoed through the large open classroom.

Without waiting for an answer, the doors were opened and the sound of footfalls could be heard crossing the classroom. Rogers' eyes grew wide for a moment as he apprised the stranger who walked into the office wearing a large overcoat and carrying a leather satchel under his left arm.

"Colonel Rogers?" the man asked as he removed his top hat. His voice had a slight trace of foreign accent that Benjamin could not quite place.

"You must be Mister Ney," he replied, standing and extending his hand.

Peter Stuart Ney was a big man in every sense of the word. In an age when the average man stood five-and-a-half feet or less, he towered at least six feet. Even under his long greatcoat, Rogers could readily see that Ney's powerful chest and shoulders matched his height. He possessed a strong, square jaw and broad forehead. His hair was reddish in colour and naturally curly, with a few sparse strands of grey. Though thinning on top, he had a distinct comb-over. It was windy outside, and while the rest of his hair was a bit dishevelled, it looked as if he had taken the time to ensure the left side of his crown was covered, as if he was trying to hide a scar or other blemish.

"Please be seated," Rogers said, gesturing towards the chair across the desk from him. "Tell me, what brings you down from Philadelphia in search of a teaching position?"

"I grew tired of the noise of the city," Ney explained.

"Can't say I blame you there," Rogers replied with a chuckle. "I've never been one for the chaos of such vast dens of humanity."

"I did just turn fifty, five days ago in fact," the tall man continued. "I would like a more...*quiet* profession for my later years." He then reached into his satchel and pulled out some documents. "Some of my credentials."

"You're French," the colonel said as he read. "That explains the accent, though I could not place its origins."

"My childhood home in Lorraine was both French and German," Ney replied. "I grew up speaking both languages from the time I was born. I also learned English as soon as I began school. During my years in the army, I travelled about so much that I suppose I was never in one place long enough to develop a thick accent."

"It says here you speak Greek and Latin," Rogers continued, not paying attention to Ney's last statement. "Splendid!"

"I confess I am a little out of practice speaking Greek," Peter stated. "However, I can write both languages proficiently. I also have a background in music."

Benjamin continued to read Ney's credentials in silence over the next few minutes before he spoke again. "Very impressive." He then nodded towards the documents. "Yet despite your extensive qualifications, I see but a single word when listing your last profession; *soldier*. No other details?"

"I worked in civil service as a young man," Peter explained, "before spending the better part of three decades in the armies of France."

"I see," the colonel said, now visually apprising this mysterious man. His commanding presence told Rogers that he must have been a man with some rank, a sergeant major, or even a colonel perhaps. Benjamin's knowledge of Revolutionary France was sparse at best. Though he did at least know the names of some of the more famous generals of the age, even if he could not put a face behind them. There was one marshal of the French Empire who shared the same last name as the mysterious stranger. If Rogers remembered correctly, he had been executed four years ago.

"You wonder if I served with Napoleon Bonaparte," Ney surmised, after allowing a few moments' silence. "The answer is yes. And if you must know, were he to return to France, I would don the uniform and stand by his side once more."

Peter's gaze almost unnerved Rogers. There was no malice about him. In fact, his demeanour seemed rather genial in stark contrast to his imposing size. But there was a bold sense of determination, of a man who had been through enough harrowing ordeals to last ten lifetimes. It may have been rather presumptuous to assume just on an expression alone, but Benjamin knew right away that Peter Stuart Ney was a man of strong convictions and fierce courage.

"Well, Bonaparte has been in exile for the better part of four years, so hopefully we would not be deprived of your services too soon," the colonel noted with a nervous chuckle. He shrugged. "Anyway, the position pays twenty dollars a month."

"A reasonable sum," Ney replied. "I take it you are accepting my application?"

"That would be a fair assessment," the colonel answered. He leaned back in his chair and folded his hands, curiosity getting the best of him. "One thing we share in common, my friend, is we've both fought against the English."

"Yes," Peter nodded, appearing uncertain as to how much he wanted to discuss such matters until the two men were better acquainted. He sought to deflect inquiries into his own past with a question. "Where did you serve?"

"Up north," Rogers replied with a nod of his head backwards. "I'm originally from Philadelphia, and despite spending the last few years in these parts I have yet to pick up the local accent. I was wounded at the Battle of Queenston Heights five years ago." He then shook his head at a series of memories. "You know, people around here like to talk about the heroics of Andrew Jackson and the thrashing he gave the redcoats at New Orleans. Well, that happened after the war was technically over, and was really our only decisive victory of the whole pointless affair."

Ney sat in silence, cracking the slightest trace of a smile. Clearly the colonel was anxious to talk about his past experiences. Peter reckoned he spoke about it constantly and was glad to have a fresh set of ears that were willing to listen.

"Who did you serve with?" Peter prodded gently, allowing the man to tell his tale, with the silent hope that he would not have to divulge his own past just yet.

"I was with the 23$^{rd}$ United States Regiment of infantry," Rogers continued. "We left with the highest of hopes, intent on either wresting eastern Canada away from King George or, in the very least, depriving his forces of supplies and bases with which to stage from. Damned internal quarrels with our senior generals, most of whom had no practical military experience at all, doomed us to failure."

"The best soldiers are useless if poorly led," Peter observed.

"What's worse, nearly half our militias simply refused to cross the border into Canada," Rogers remembered. "I'll never forget the crashing volleys of British muskets as they cut us to pieces; the deafening roar, the acrid smoke, the screams of the wounded. I was shot in the leg in the very first salvo and was among the fortunate ones who were evacuated across the Niagara. Tell me, *Mister* Ney— for I do not know what your rank in Napoleon's army was—did you ever have to face down the barrels of relentless musket fire from those damned redcoats?"

Peter said nothing, but sat in quiet contemplation, his eyes seeing not Colonel Benjamin Rogers, but another time and place altogether. Suddenly, his left arm started to ache…

British counterattack at the Battle of Queenston Heights

# Chapter II: The Guard is Broken

### Field of Waterloo, Belgium
### 18 June 1815

Napoleon Reviews the Imperial Guard

*I have you now, Wellington! At last, I have beaten you!*

These were the inner thoughts of Michel Ney, Marshal of France, as he stood inside the courtyard of La Haye Sainte, the farmhouse the Anglo-Allied army had been using as its central stronghold since the Battle of Waterloo commenced. Knowing its strategic value, and understanding that its capture would cause Wellington's centre to collapse, Napoleon had been utterly relentless in sending assault after assault against its walls. Though relieved that it had fallen at last, Ney was appalled by the cost in lives. It was now 7 o'clock in the evening, and the battle had raged for the past eight hours with neither side gaining the advantage. Waves of imperial soldiers had attacked the three British strongholds all afternoon. They had suffered horrific losses in the process as they advanced across open ground; their redcoat adversaries, along with their more numerous Dutch and Germanic allies, either digging in on a long ridge or firing from walls and rooftops.

The epic clash between Wellington and Napoleon, arguably two of the greatest military leaders to have ever lived, had ground to a bloody standstill until this moment. The future of France and, indeed, the entire world, hinged on this battle. Ney knew the fate of the battle would be settled once the farmhouse that served as the strongpoint of the British centre fell. He rushed through the gate, his sword held high, as Green-jacketed sharpshooters from the British 95th Rifles, their ammunition expended, rushed down from the walls and into the courtyard. With escape impossible, they were now engaged in brutal hand-to-hand fighting with overwhelming numbers of Ney's men. The French, having lost so many of their friends to the venerable sharpshooters, were now exacting their vengeance with close-range musket fire and bayonet.

As he stood next to the smashed in gate, French soldiers continuing to pour into the outer courtyard with shouts of 'Vive le France!', the marshal stopped for a moment and took a deep breath. The forty-six year old Ney had spent the last twenty-eight years of his life in military service to France. He began humbly enough as a private, rising up through the enlisted and non-commissioned ranks before accepting a commission with a subsequent promotion to général de brigade in just nine years. Now général de division and a Marshal of France, his tactical savvy and extreme bravery had earned him the accolades of both friend and foe alike. He had won countless victories for his nation and was wounded numerous times, always contemptuous of his enemy and devoid of any fear of death. His uniform was scorched and tattered, and he stretched out his left arm, where a fearful scar between his shoulder and elbow, from an injury 'won' over twenty years before, still ached constantly.

The fighting had been savage, and Ney seemed to always be at the heart of it. He'd lost four horses that day, one during an ill-fated cavalry charge that had seen most of Napoleon's mounted regiments shot to pieces by British infantry squares, and his body was covered in fresh gashes and contusions. His ears rang from the continuous concussion of cannon and musketry, his eyes were bloodshot, and his very soul wrecked by the gory sights of the dead, as well as the incessant cries of anguish from the gravely wounded. Yet for all that he had endured, and despite his near exhaustion, Marshal Ney was once again proving unstoppable. There was only one thing left to do, and that was to finish his old nemesis, Wellington.

"Hold this position," he told his aide, a Polish colonel named Lehmanowski, as he mounted his fifth horse of the day. "The English centre has fallen; now is the time for the final stroke of the hammer."

"Very good, sir," the colonel acknowledged, as Ney rode down the gentle slope. After ten minutes of riding through the quagmire brought on by constant rains—for indeed, the day of battle was the only one of sunshine they had seen in a week—churned up still more by cannon shot and littered with dead and dying men, he arrived outside the house known as La Belle Alliance. It was here that Napoleon made his headquarters, and the Emperor of the French was dictating what would be his final orders of the battle.

Clouds of acrid smoke obscured the emperor's view of the ridge, which made assessing the tactical situation more difficult as the day wore on. Off to his left, the roof of the farmhouse at the Château d'Hougoumont burned, casting an eerie glow through the haze. That stronghold, regrettably, was still held by the British, having cost thousands of French lives in futile assaults. Strategically, though, Hougoumont meant nothing, provided the French managed to capture La Haye Sainte.

The battle had been extremely bloody and exhausting, and was further compounded by the arrival of Wellington's Prussian allies under Marshal Blucher on the French right flank. Napoleon smashed their army just two days before at Ligny, yet it appeared the old German Cossack still had some fight left in him. Thankfully, the remnants of Blucher's army had been arriving at Waterloo piecemeal throughout the day, a few companies at a time, and had been held off by one of Napoleon's corps at a stronghold called Plancenoit. But now their numbers were growing, and Napoleon knew his flank would be overwhelmed before long. He *had* to break Wellington's centre if he was to win this day! Of course, he had been in such precarious positions before, worse, in fact. One crowning example was the Battle of Marengo, which had taken place almost exactly fifteen years prior. The emperor was famous for saying, "I lost the battle at 5 o'clock, but I won it back again at 7!"

"Sire, La Haye Sainte is ours!" Ney said excitedly as he rode up. "Give me the Imperial Guard, and I will smash Wellington once and for all!"

Despite the fact that his army was completely exhausted, with casualties exceeding half his total strength, the emperor had resolutely kept his elite troops in reserve. The Imperial Guard were not only the best soldiers in the French Empire, and indeed the entire world, their appearance alone would have a grave psychological impact on their enemies. With the Anglo-Allied centre fallen, coupled by the incessant attacks by the Prussians on their right flank, Napoleon knew it was time to unleash the Guard. The British and their allies were completely exhausted and nearly shattered, having committed their own reserves hours ago. Once Wellington broke, Blucher would have no option but to withdraw or capitulate. Eight hours of relentless ferocity, and now it came down to a period of a few minutes that would decide all.

"You shall have them," the emperor nodded. "The Young Guard is deployed on our right flank with Lobau's corps, holding the Prussians in check at Plancenoit. The Middle Guard will lead the assault, with the Old Guard in support. Once the Prussians see that the English and Dutch are beaten, they will succumb. Now go! Make Wellington feel that which he has never suffered; break him and let him know the ignominy of defeat!"

Ney saluted and rode the short distance to where the columns of the Imperial Guard were marching up the road. By God, they were a magnificent sight! While most of the French army had been in a bloody grind since late that morning with Wellington's forces, the emperor's best troops had been waiting well behind the lines for this moment. They marched in perfect step, muskets shouldered with bayonets fixed, free arms swinging sharply. They wore long blue frockcoats with white belts crisscrossing their chests. Atop each head was a tall bearskin hat with a brass plate at the base. Most, especially the older veterans of the Old Guard, had thick, bushy moustaches that had become a symbol of their status as much as the bearskin hats.

At their head marched Général de Brigade Jean-Paul Poret de Morvan, in his resplendent officer's uniform with bicorn hat. By contrast to many of his men, he was clean-shaven, as were most of the officers. The general had chosen to fight on foot instead of on horseback. He drew his sword as the marshal rode up to him, giving a loud shout of, *"Vive l'Empereur!"*

"Soldiers of the Imperial Guard!" Ney shouted. "Now is your time! On that ridge is our destiny! *Vive la France!*"

Général de Brigade Paul-Jean Poret de Morvan

The bands struck up with their fifes and drums as the pride of France marched briskly past La Belle Alliance. The emperor himself was now astride his horse, riding at the head of their columns to the shouts and cheers of his men. Mounted beside him was his chief-of-staff, Marshal Nicolas Soult. Soult and Ney were close friends, with Michel expressing early on in the campaign that Nicolas' talents were wasted serving as chief-of-staff. Up to that point, Soult was one of the few who had ever even come close to beating Wellington and should have been commanding a corps, or a division in the least!

The music was temporarily drowned out in the horrendous crash of French cannon; hundreds of guns trained on the short ridge, pummelling the Anglo-Allied lines. Incessant rains had saturated the ground for the past week, so there was much doubt as to just how effective the steel round shot would be. Ney also knew Wellington's favoured tactic of utilizing the reverse slope to shield his men from the effects of cannon fire, as well as a means of masking his numbers. Two days before, at Ligny, the Prussians had left themselves exposed in the open, allowing Napoleon to mass his artillery and blast them to pieces. Had the Duke employed the same tactics, the battle would have been over within an hour and the Armee du Nord would be marching on to Brussels. Ney shook his head and pushed out all other thoughts from his mind as he scanned the ridge and mentally prepared himself for the assault. It did, in fact, appear that Wellington was beaten, yet the marshal forced himself to remain focused and not grow overconfident. After all, just hours earlier, he had thought the Duke's army was on the run, and when he led the cavalry pursuit, they'd run right into thousands of British soldiers in infantry squares hiding behind the ridge!

Ney's mind raced as he thought back to the previous battles he'd fought against the Duke. The two men had faced each other on several occasions during the Peninsular War, and while Ney had bloodied the Duke's forces a number of times, he'd never gained that elusive victory. The closest he had come was just two days prior, at Quatre Bras. While Napoleon had taken the right wing of his army to smash the Prussians, Ney was charged with preventing Wellington from reinforcing them, as well as taking the crossroads at Quatre Bras. The action began as a minor engagement with Dutch militia before escalating into a bloody grind as Wellington's British and Hanoverian divisions rushed to their aid. Ney was still bitter that Napoleon had diverted an entire corps of his army to come to Ligny, depriving the marshal of 20,000 men that would have given him the decisive blow needed to completely rout the English. As it was, the errant corps received conflicting countermanding orders from both Ney and Napoleon and, as such, engaged in neither battle. While the marshal lamented the lost opportunity, he knew Wellington was in the same predicament, as his entire II Corps had still been on the march and, indeed, only a few elements had even arrived in time to fight at Waterloo.

None of that mattered now. Battalions of the Imperial Guard were deploying from road march into rows of attack columns, advancing up the gentle slope. And with the collapse of the Anglo-Allied centre, it was now only a matter of finishing them off. This time Wellington *had* to be broken! The fifes had ceased, yet the drums continued to sound their ominous cadence as soldiers of the Guard shouted, *'Vive la France!',* in conjunction to the drumbeat.

As they neared the top of the ridge, Marshal Ney's eyes grew wide and he gave a sinister grin. He spotted a man on a horse by a large tree in the distance, wearing a blue greatcoat and bicorn hat, carrying a telescope in his right hand. As the advancing Guard drew closer, Ney recognized him to be none other than Wellington himself, come out to meet his vanquishers it seemed. The Duke appeared to be practically alone, only a couple of staff officers were mounted beside him, as if the rest of his army had already deserted him.

Ney's eyes became focused with wrath; he would finally have his vengeance on the one man who had bested him so many times before! "You're mine now, Wellington!" he hissed.

The lead columns of the Imperial Guard continued to march in step, their pace quickening slightly. No doubt many were eyeing the prize of their enemy commander-in-chief.

Then to the marshal's horror and bemusement, out of the tall grass rose a single British officer in a uniform of the 1st Regiment of Foot Guards. The grass and weeds had obscured the man from Ney's vision. Now he was so close the marshal could clearly hear the man shout over this shoulder in English, *"Front line…up!"*

A long line of British redcoats, arrayed in two ranks, quickly stood, as if they had sprung up from the very ground itself. No more than thirty feet from the advancing Imperial Guard, they opened fire in a crashing volley of musketry that blew apart the lead elements of the French battalions in a bursting array of blood and gore. Men screamed in both surprise and agony as their bodies, and those of their closest friends, were shattered by the large calibre musketballs.

*"Second line…up!"*

As quickly as they had stood and fired, the English soldiers knelt down, with a subsequent line rising up and unleashing a fearsome volley, rapidly followed by a third. Within seconds the front ranks of the advancing columns were shot to pieces. Hundreds of guardsmen lay sprawled in the grass. Their companions having to step on or over their mutilated bodies. This caused the advance to stall. The columns breaking apart as the survivors negotiated the gory obstacle.

The agony of the wounded, with their broken limbs and ruptured guts, was compounded by the utter shock they had suffered. The British should have been beaten! Whereas a few seconds before, Marshal Ney and the Imperial Guard had sneered at the Duke of

Wellington in triumph, he now watched in horror as walls of redcoats continued to rise from the tall grass and fire close-range volleys into the still advancing French columns. The English were spacing the barrages enough so that when the third line of companies fired, those in front were finishing reloading and rising up to unleash once more. In the half minute it took for the French to realize what they'd run into, a total of six rolling volleys had completely annihilated their lead ranks. Individual soldiers were starting to return fire, but in a column it was impossible for the French to mass their musketry against the British lines. Each time a wall of redcoats rose from the grass to open fire, a few were felled by shots from the advancing French; yet the English volleys were concentrated, with so many weapons firing at once that entire ranks of the Imperial Guard were slaughtered with each salvo.

Ney's horse cried out as it collapsed, hit several times in the latest wave of musket fire. Somehow the Marshal himself was not shot, and he landed hard upon the rocks, jarring his left arm once more. Dazed, with the symphony of musketry echoing relentlessly, he struggled to his feet. He was still in a state of shock as he tried to regain his bearings. The Guard continued to advance, yet they were now buckling under the merciless onslaught of British firepower. As Ney clawed his way up the slope, which was slick with blood and gore, covered in bodies of slain and terribly wounded men, he found General Morvan trying to pull himself from a pile of the badly maimed who had fallen on him.

"By God, Marshal!" the general cried as Ney pulled him from the heap. "Where did they come from?"

Morvan, who was among the most fearless men Ney had ever known, looked like a man whose very soul had been crushed. His bicorn hat was gone, his sword broken in two. The general's face and uniform were covered in blood, though one could not tell if it was his or that of his men. Another eruption of British fire smashed into their ranks. Men, all around the marshal and his general, screaming as they fell.

"Come, Paul-Jean!" Ney shouted, addressing the general by his given name. "We must rise up for our men to follow us!"

The Guards general nodded, though his expression was vacant, etched with horror. Even Marshal Ney, who had survived the horrific Russian campaign, could not have been prepared for the sight of the

Imperial Guard's rapid destruction. The volleys from the British lines were so close and unrelenting. With each burst, it looked as if an entire rank of French columns was blown apart. No matter how bad a battle went, it was unheard of for units to suffer 100% casualties. Yet he was certain that in this close and horrific mauling, entire companies were lost in each musket storm.

*"Maintain the advance!"* Ney shouted as he struggled past wavering ranks of men, some of whom were returning fire or stopping to reload their muskets. Refusing to allow his emotions to get the best of him, the marshal paused and made a quick assessment of their foes. They were spread thin, and he reckoned there were less than a thousand total redcoats facing them, barely one third of his own strength. If they could just close the distance and engage with the bayonet, the British would break. The Guards were beginning to waver and the distance, which had been perhaps thirty feet at the start of the engagement, was now growing. Those soldiers who found themselves in the front ranks faltered as more of their companions were shot down. Ney knew he had to rally his men, lest the unthinkable happen and the Imperial Guard broke.

"We almost have them!" he shouted. "Fall upon their lines and carry this day!" He then climbed upon a rock, willing himself to be shot down if it should allow him to inspire the Guard to make a final thrust into what he knew to be Wellington's last stand. *"Men of the Imperial Guard, you know me! I am Ney...Ney, Marshal of France!"*

His selfless act led to a renewed battle cry from the Guard, and they pressed forward. It was not to be. For as the encouraged men reformed and advanced past the marshal, the British volleys smashed into them once more. The bravest men who led from the front fell, screaming in terrible pain as musket shot ripped into their bodies. Compressed into their columns, the momentum of those in front, who were in a state of panic, pressed against those behind them and all began to stumble back down the slope. As they retreated, the rolling volleys of the British soldiers suddenly stopped. Ney surmised their enemies were out of ammunition, for his force was still within range, yet the salvos had ceased.

*"Stand, men of the Imperial Guard!"* he bellowed as he walked amongst the ranks of his men. "The Guard dies, but it does not retreat nor does it surrender!"

Having time to regain their composure, soldiers began to reform the columns. Ney, deprived of a horse and not even bothering to draw his sword, sprinted from one battalion to the next, attempting to rally the survivors to assault once more. He could now see the advancing British lines as they trod through the gory mess of the massacre they had unleashed. Their regimental colours and the hateful Union flag were silhouetted against the skyline, which was red with the onset of evening. Night was coming soon, and the red sky seemed to poetically accent the amount of blood spilled this day. Ney was heartened when he noted how few the British numbers were.

"Look!" he said. "The English advance on us with less than half our strength! Their bayonets are forward, their ammunition spent! Stand your ground, Middle Guard! One more push and we'll have them beaten!"

*"Vive la France!"* General Morvan shouted, which was echoed by the men of the Imperial Guard.

Anxious now to avenge their slain and shattered friends, many of whom had served together for nearly twenty years, they gave a loud battle cry and brandished their bayonets once more. Sporadic shots rang out from their ranks and the advancing British soldiers quickly knelt down as several of their numbers fell. There was no return fire, which confirmed Ney's suspicions that their ammunition was exhausted. His men were regrouping, with their officers readying them to advance once more.

Ney's relief soon turned to dismay and defeat as a crash of musketry tore into the left flank of the reformed Imperial Guard. Men cried out in surprise and pain as they were cut down. Officers and their sergeants quickly attempted to form up their men and return fire, but it was proving to be in vain.

*"Merde!"* a soldier shouted. "We've been flanked!"

The attacking force was the 52nd Oxfordshire, the largest British regiment on the field that day. With well over a thousand men, they had sustained relatively light casualties when compared to the savagery the rest of the Anglo-Allied Army had suffered. And so, they were relatively fresh with a full complement of ammunition. Their volleys were measured and deliberate, each slamming home into the now-exhausted and demoralized files of the French. Green-jacketed sharpshooters from the 60th and 95th Rifles were also joining the fray, their long range shots deliberately aimed at officers and NCOs of the Imperial Guard.

There was now nothing that Ney or Morvan could do; their men saw only death around them, and even the bravest could no longer stand in the face of such relentless destruction.

"Lost!" a captain shouted. "All is lost!" As if in penance for his cowardly speech, the officer was torn to pieces in the subsequent volley of musket fire from the Oxfordshire, his face and torso ripped apart as he fell, twitching violently, gouts of blood saturating the already sodden earth.

"What can we do, marshal?" Morvan asked, all hope lost in his eyes.

"Die," Ney replied calmly.

Yet neither man would meet his end this day, as they were practically carried along in the waves of fleeing men. Trumpets were sounding up on the ridge, with regiments of Wellington's army now advancing of their own volition. Off to their right, the French soldiers who had battled through horrific odds in the taking of La Haye Sainte now abandoned their hard-won conquest, as they fled for their lives.

Night was fast approaching, and as the remnants of the Imperial Guard were swept away towards La Belle Alliance, Ney knew he had one last duty to perform. He needed to organize what was left into a viable rear guard in order to try and save as many lives as he could. Individual companies held their ground around their broken cannon and caissons as they were swarmed by British soldiers and their allies. Ignoring the pleas of the advancing redcoats to surrender, many simply allowed themselves to be shot or bayonetted by their foes. Ney shoved his way through the chaos, determined to do his duty to the very last.

"Where is the emperor?" he asked, as he came upon Napoleon's chief-of-staff, Marshal Nicolas Soult, who was quickly mounting his horse.

"I had him sent from here," Soult replied, his face streaked with tears. "He cursed my name as a dozen men, under my orders, spirited him into his carriage. But I could not let the English, or worse the Prussians take him."

"You did the right thing, Nicolas," Ney replied with a tired nod. "Our duty was to the emperor, and now I must organize what remains to form a rear guard to ensure the safe retreat of the army."

"What army?" Soult asked. "The Guard has been shot to pieces, the Prussians have taken the right flank at Plancenoit, and the British now sweep the field to our front. Those who can flee are doing so, yet there is no order to be had. The rest are either dead or fast becoming prisoners of Wellington and Blucher."

"Damn it all," Ney swore quietly. He then looked back and ascertained all that his friend and fellow marshal had said. Clouds of bitter smoke hung over the battlefield, adding to the ethereal feel of it all as the sun set slowly in the west, to the left of the French Army.

"It is over for us, Michel," Soult replied, dejectedly. "France has fallen, and she will not rise again."

As Ney nodded in acknowledgement, Soult spurred his horse away from the scene of death that still played out before them. Prussian cavalry were now appearing in large numbers, and the marshal knew they would be the ones to conduct the pursuit; Wellington's mounted troops having been savaged and rendered ineffective during the battle.

Ney calmly walked the field, finding any officers and NCOs who had not completely lost their minds and compelled them to reform their men into battle lines. The Prussian horsemen would cut down or trample any stragglers they came across. The only way to ensure survival was to present a bristling front of muskets and bayonets to keep them at bay. There would be no pursuit from Wellington's army, as they were completely spent.

And so, as the broken remnants of the Armee du Nord slowly backed away from the death and destruction that was the Battle of Waterloo, the glow of the burning rooftop at Hougoumont in the distance flickered sinisterly. And just like during the Russian Campaign, Marshal Michel Ney was the last to leave the field that day.

Prussian soldiers (right) overwhelming the French defenders at Plancenoit

## Chapter III: End of a Dynasty

Cheraw, South Carolina
3 June 1821
\*\*\*

The sun shone brightly on that early June morning. Birds chirped loudly and the smell of fresh rain and flowering trees filled the air. The school term was set to end soon, and the citizens of the small community of Cheraw had grown collectively fond of the headmaster, who was now completing his third year of teaching. During the spring following Peter Ney's arrival, the first steamboats had come upriver, bringing much in the way of trade and prosperity to the tiny community. Corn, cotton, tobacco, rice, and indigo from the local plantations could now be exported far and wide. With the influx of wealth came well-to-do families who wanted the finest of educations for their sons and, in some cases, daughters.

In just three years, Peter Stuart Ney's reputation as a teacher spread throughout the surrounding counties. The enigmatic Frenchman possessed both academic and real-world experience that his students found fascinating. His textbooks, particularly those detailing the histories of France and greater Europe, were covered in notes and scribbles; 'corrections', as he called them.

Colonel Benjamin Rogers had given Peter lodgings on his plantation, and while the Frenchman had grown quite close to Benjamin and his family, the colonel still knew very little about his friend's past. After their first conversation, Peter never again mentioned his time as a soldier of Napoleon, although his military history tended to surface itself in many ways, particularly when relating to his teaching style. He made his students stand at the position of attention when conducting recitations, something the colonel rather enjoyed. He was also a very strict disciplinarian, yet fair. Failure to stand at attention during recitations, or if a student spoke out of turn when his peers were speaking, would bring a sharp rap from the headmaster's walking stick. Given his agility to mount and dismount his horse, as well as his physical prowess, students joked that Mister Ney did not need his stick for walking but for disciplining unruly charges. Peter also ingrained his young charges with his personal sense of integrity and honour. If a student committed an infraction, he would often report himself to the schoolmaster.

Then there was the incident a few months prior, where a young militia officer, who was rumoured to be a master swordsman, had come to teach the students fencing and had, in jest, challenged Peter to a match. The schoolmaster, refusing the sword that was offered to him and instead using his walking stick, disarmed his opponent with incredible speed and precision. The humbled swordsman bowed and told the students, "You do not need me, for you already have a master swordsman amongst you."

Though strict, he was also very fair with his students when dolling out both punishment and reward. They, in turn, spoke his highest praises. Peter, in terms that sounded more like he was speaking of soldiers than school boys, often said that a leader's true worth was measured in the loyalty he garnered from his subordinates. Whatever mysteries surrounded his past, the people of Cheraw had long since welcomed Peter Stuart Ney as one of their own.

The schoolmaster had intended to keep this day brief. His pupils needed to study for their final exams in two days, and so he was content to give a short lecture on the political processes of various European nations. This subject would not be graded this term, but rather was meant to expand the young minds to think beyond the politics and governing of their small communities.

"Excuse me, sir," one of the young men in his class said, raising his hand as Peter stepped up to the speaker's podium.

"Yes?"

"I brought a newspaper I thought you might find interesting, in regard to today's subject," the lad explained holding up the rolled paper.

Peter gave a gentle smile and nodded, extending his hand and accepting the roll from the young man. His eyes grew wide and his hands began to tremble as he read the headline:

## *Napoleon Dead!*
## *Former Emperor of the French dies in exile on Saint Helena...*

The gathered students thought it heat or simply exhaustion, but whatever it was, their headmaster's face turned pale, and his eyes rolled into the back of his head as he collapsed. The town doctor was promptly summoned, though he determined it was overwork and nothing more. A carriage took Peter to his quarters on the Rogers plantation, where the doctor recommended he rest up for the remainder of the day. During a brief conversation with Benjamin Rogers, who came to check on his friend that evening, Peter assured him he was better, and he would be in class on the morrow to oversee the end of term exams.

"The exams are in two days," Benjamin noted. "Surely your students can take a day to study on their own while their teacher takes a day to recuperate."

"No," Peter replied, shaking his head. "A leader does not rest while his men toil. Besides, I would rather my students were able to focus on studying, rather than concerning themselves with my wellbeing."

At this, the colonel nodded and left the matter alone. He then said a servant would bring Peter his evening meal and that he would see him on the morrow. As soon as Benjamin left, Peter produced a small knife from under his bedding. He closed his eyes, his hands trembling as a single tear rolled down his cheek.

The next morning came, yet there was no sign of the headmaster. One of the students, the same young man who had brought the newspaper the previous morning, exited the large classroom and happened upon Colonel Rogers, who was on his way to visit the school.

"Ah, young man!" Benjamin said. "Ready for your exams tomorrow morning?"

"Indeed we are, sir," the lad replied. "Provided we have a teacher to administer them to us."

"Mister Ney not there this morning?"

"No, sir," the student responded.

"Well, this is most troubling," the colonel said with a furrowed brow. "I spoke with Mister Ney last evening, and he assured me he was feeling better and that he would be here early." His mouth twisted as he tried to contemplate what this could mean.

In the three years since taking over as headmaster for the Cheraw School, Peter had never been so much as a minute late to class. His fainting spell the day before had been the only issue to arise during his tenure. Finally, Benjamin, fearing something dreadful was amiss, nodded and said to the young man, "Come with me."

Thankfully, his carriage was close, and it was but a few minutes along the dusty road to his nearby plantation. Slaves could be seen toiling in the fields. The young student remembered hearing his schoolmaster talk in depth about slavery, stating it was the one thing in his adopted land that he found abhorrent. On several occasions he had made mention of the fact that in France, King Louis X had abolished the practice five hundred years before, and it had disappeared altogether from the European continent. Even the British had refused to recognize slavery within England in 1569 and, though it still existed in many of its distant colonies such as India, it was a rapidly dying practice within their empire. Peter Ney had sometimes lamented, with great passion, how much it pained him to see the land which professed loudest to be one of free men was, in fact, the last bastion of human bondage in the civilized world. The plight of those poor souls who laboured in the afternoon sun troubled the young man as his teacher's words rang loudly in his head.

"Those who would take away the free will of men have forfeited the right to their own," he had said in one instance.

Strangely enough, his abolitionist views had not brought him into conflict with his host, Benjamin Rogers. Indeed, the two were strong friends and the colonel was now gravely concerned over the eccentric Frenchman.

A servant took the reins as he and the young student made their way up an outside staircase to Peter's quarters on the upper landing. The colonel banged on the door, calling out his friend's name, but to no avail.

"Peter?" he shouted for what must have been the tenth time. He then fumbled for his keys and, after a few moments, forced his way into the room. The sight horrified both he and the lad with him.

"Send for the doctor!" he said, shoving the young man towards the steps.

He descended quickly, shouting for one of Rogers' slaves to take him to the doctor.

Inside, Benjamin was horrified by what he saw. Peter lay face down on the floor in a pool of coagulating blood. The colonel knelt next to him, paying no mind to the blood that now stained his own trousers. A small knife lay next to the schoolmaster, and the side of his neck bore a jagged gash, showing that his hand had been shaking terribly when he attempted to sever the artery. The blood had, thankfully, clotted. And though his face was ghostly white, he was still breathing, albeit very shallowly. Benjamin, remembering back to his days in war and having witnessed such fearful injuries, pulled a sheet from the bed and tore it to make a compression bandage which he placed over the wound. He carefully rolled his friend onto his side, keeping pressure on the wound and ensuring Peter was still breathing.

An hour passed before the young man finally returned with the town doctor. The older gentleman had seen much in the way of horrific trauma, though even he was shocked by the sight. The amount of blood alone convinced him Peter should be dead.

"He's alive, but I'm not sure for how long," Benjamin replied. His hands, shirtsleeves, and trousers were completely saturated.

"Hold his head," the doctor directed, opening his bag. Through no small effort, he managed to stitch the terrible wound. When he, at last, gave a sigh of relief, Benjamin allowed himself to breathe easy. With Peter lying comfortably in his bed, a large bandage around his neck, the doctor finally left. Benjamin vowed to remain by his friend's side until it was clear as to why he tried to take his own life. The schoolteacher slept all the next day, leading to a postponement of the end-of-term exams for his students, and it was the following evening when Peter finally spoke.

"Napoleon is dead," he said quietly, in an answer to Benjamin's unasked question. "My last hope is gone."

"Last hope of what?" the colonel inquired.

Though they had not spoken about Peter's past regarding the deposed Emperor of the French, he knew something from Ney's history related to Napoleon's death.

"It means I can never go home," Peter explained. "I came to America because, in France, my life was forfeit after the empire fell. As long as Napoleon lived, I had a glimmer of faith that I would be able to see my wife and sons once more. That hope is now gone. Forgive me, my friend, for I am sorry to have caused you such needless distress. I sought the coward's way out by attempting to take my own life. Such is unbecoming of a soldier. Thank God my hand was unsteady, or else I should have succeeded."

"You were clearly assailed by doubts," Benjamin conjectured. "We have all seen how steady your hand is with a fencing blade, and I suspect if you truly meant to die, you would have done so."

"Yes," Peter nodded, "I suppose that is true, too. And that should assuage you of any suspicions you have that I may attempt this again."

"Give me your word as a soldier and as my friend, that you will never more try to depart this world by your own hand. The good Lord will come for you in his own time."

The colonel extended his hand, which Peter clasped with surprising strength given his extensive blood loss and weakened state.

"God gave me a second chance at life," he replied. "It would be an insult to Him if I were to throw away the gift." Benjamin thought Peter's reference to a second chance was in light of this recent incident, yet the Frenchman was, in reality, referring to a time from his past, during what was really another life altogether.

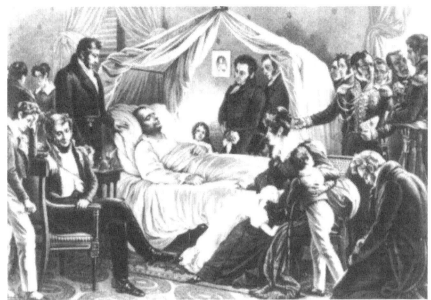
Napoleon on his deathbed, 5 May 1821

Peter Stuart Ney kept his word to his friends. Nevermore did he make attempts to harm himself; and while the incident was never forgotten, out of respect it was never spoken of in his presence. Three days later, he oversaw the exams of his students and brought the term to an end. And yet, he was clearly changed afterwards. An unfortunate consequence of the news regarding Napoleon's death was that Peter had taken to finding consolation in drink. Sometimes, after too many glasses of whiskey or gin, he would tell wild stories, a few times referring to himself as a 'Marshal of the Empire'. When sober, he would dismiss these as drunken attempts at humour, further stating that he had been a humble soldier and nothing more. On several occasions, Peter lay in a near stupor and could be heard calling out a woman's name. Though he had freely told friends he was married, he had never mentioned his wife's name. Yet, during times of too much drink, he would call out the name 'Aglae'.

The fall term began, and once school was in session, Peter became the consummate professional. He curtailed his drinking during this time and appeared to be himself once more. Then, one cold winter evening, the effects of drink came to add yet another layer of mystery to this eccentric Frenchman.

It was Christmas break, and Peter was enjoying the company at the house of one of their neighbours, a former colonel named Houston and his family. The old schoolteacher had consumed nearly half a bottle of whiskey by himself, to say nothing of the copious amounts of claret he had drank prior to and during dinner. He excused himself, saying he needed to step out and let the winter air wake him up some. After a few minutes, Houston went to check on his friend, only to find Peter lying on the ground, fast asleep, with a thin layer of snow forming on him. Houston chuckled and shook his head before summoning his manservant to help him lift the rather large Frenchman onto his horse.

"What, you throw the Duke of Elchingen on a horse like a sack?!" Peter protested sharply as he woke up suddenly. He soon passed out again, and nothing else was said. Soon the schoolmaster was at home and fast asleep in his bed, though his words confused Houston greatly.

The following afternoon he spoke to Benjamin Rogers about it.

"What do you know about the Duke of Elchingen?" Houston asked.

"Not a thing," Benjamin replied. "A European peerage, I'm assuming." He chuckled, "So our good schoolmaster says he's a duke, does he? Well, he's said many fanciful things when he's had a few too many drinks. We all have."

"Honestly, I didn't know what to make of it." Houston shrugged. "I mean, we know so very little about him, and he rarely ever talks about his previous life in France. For all we know, he could have been a prince or a peasant."

"He's too well educated to have been a peasant," Rogers replied. He noted the concerned expression on his fellow colonel's face. "What is it?"

"I did a little research of my own this morning," Houston replied. "I found some information in a recently published book about the French nobility under Napoleon. The thing is, the Duke of Elchingen died six years ago."

# Chapter IV: Last Gasps of the Empire

The Chamber of Peers
Paris, France
22 June 1815

The Chamber of Peers at the Palais du Luxembourg, Paris

Four days had passed since the disaster at Waterloo. Prussian cavalry had chased the fleeing remnants of Napoleon's army long into the night after the battle, with thousands being either killed or captured. With Marshal Soult retiring to the capitol, another marshal, Emmanuel Grouchy, had triumphed over Prussian forces at Wavre the day after Waterloo. Napoleon had been rushed back to Paris, where word of the disaster had already caused the citizens to panic. A handful of cavalry from the Imperial Guard arrived with the emperor, though none of the surviving regiments of infantry had yet made the near two hundred mile trek from Waterloo to Paris.

It was impossible to tell just how many remained, for there was no order once the Imperial Guard had broken. Ney's rear guard had done their duty and prevented the entire army from being wiped out, with the survivors joining Marshal Grouchy during the return march. Regrettably, he had been completely unaware of Napoleon's crushing defeat and, as such, his victory at Wavre proved too late to salvage the campaign.

With much of Europe engaged in hostilities with France, the loss at Waterloo was proving catastrophic, for the entire war hinged on Napoleon defeating Blucher and Wellington. The approach of the Austrian and Russian forces had been ground to a halt by the reconstituted French armies in the east. However, with the *Armee du Nord* practically destroyed, and Napoleon himself suffering such an ignominious defeat, the road to Paris from the north was wide open for the British and Prussians.

Ney, having secured a rear guard for the retreating army, returned to Paris as well. It was early morning, just before sunrise, when he returned home. He had not slept in days, his uniform was burned, ripped, and soiled, his hair dishevelled, and his face wrought with both filth and anguish. His youngest son shrieked at the sight of him as he walked into the entryway of their home. Ney resembled a frightful monster more than the boy's father.

"My God, Michel," Aglae said, rushing into the room at the sound of the lad's cry.

"Napoleon is finished," Ney said plainly. "The Armee du Nord has been destroyed. The English and Prussians will be in Paris within a week. I must wash and prepare to address the Chamber of Peers."

Aglae, her eyes, at first, wet with sorrow at the news, quickly composed herself. Her husband had his duties to perform, and so did she. The children were ushered away, and she had her maidservant bring the marshal's finest dress uniform to her. Aglae took it upon herself to help bathe her husband.

As she helped him out of his tattered clothes, she quickly took note of the fresh injuries he had sustained. She sighed quietly as she helped lower him into his bath. As he let the heated waters cleanse him, Aglae leaned her husband's head back and kissed him on the forehead before proceeding to shave him. As she ran the razor over his face, clearing away the stubble and grime, Ney's eyes shut for what seemed like the first time in a week. He needed to rest his mind as much as possible before he addressed the Chambers.

They had been married for nearly thirteen years, and in all that time Aglae wondered just how much of it they had spent together. She recalled the immense pride she felt in the fall of 1805 when, after his crushing victory over the Austrians, Ney was named *Duc d'Elchingen* or *Duke of Elchingen*. The next several years would be marked by near-continuous warfare; first against the Russians, then the Portuguese, Spanish, British, then the Russians once more, and finally what was known as the Sixth Coalition. In all that time, Aglae could not count the number of times she had awoken in the middle of the night, sweaty and in a panic, thinking her dear husband had met a gruesome death on some foreign battlefield. So many of her friends, all wives of Napoleon's officers, had been made widows over the years. She always heard tales of her husband's almost fanatical bravery, which, though it made her proud, she often wondered how long it would be before she joined the throngs of mourning women wearing black.

And yet, in just the little he had said since returning home the hour before, Aglae surmised that at last it may finally be over. What the future would then hold for her husband if, in fact, this was to be the end of Napoleon, she could not say. Regardless, even defeat was more preferable to many than continuous death. The coming weeks would bring even greater sorrow, as the majority of the Armee du Nord failed to return home. Wives, children, family, and friends would be in a state of shock and despair, not knowing whether their loved ones had been killed or captured. For Aglae Ney, she was grateful as she helped bathe and shave her husband who was among the living.

The emperor was to address the Chamber of Peers later that afternoon on the $22^{nd}$. His hope was to use their success in the east to rally the people, along with the remnants of his *Grande Armee* to repel the invaders who now threatened Paris itself. Napoleon reckoned that he had suffered a setback and nothing more. The Austrians and Russians were stopped, and the campaign in Belgium had netted him two victories at Ligny and Wavre, one tactical draw at Quatre Bras, with his only defeat being at Waterloo itself. Yet, even the emperor did not yet comprehend just how much of his army had been lost.

Ney had arrived early and taken the opportunity to address the Chambers first, before either Napoleon or his brother, Lucien, arrived. The Marshal of France, who fought in more battles than any could remember, and who had one time gone as far as to shoulder a musket and stand on the firing line during the desperate fighting at the Battle of Borodino during the Russian campaign of 1812, had now determined no more sons of France should die in a war that was clearly lost.

Ney also understood that his time to speak was now, before his influence waned completely. He knew the royalists already wanted him dead for betraying King Louis and re-joining the emperor's cause; though, something the marshal did not know, was that Napoleon was already blaming him for the disastrous defeat at Waterloo. Until the end of his days, Bonaparte would place the fault squarely on Michel Ney for not crushing Wellington at Quatre Bras, like Napoleon had the Prussians at Ligny. Furthermore, he blamed Ney for the loss of his cavalry at Waterloo, though this was understandable, as Ney had misjudged a reposition of Wellington's forces as a retreat and ordered an all-out cavalry charge without waiting for infantry support. What was most unfair, though, was the emperor even went so far as to attribute the destruction of the Imperial Guard to the marshal.

Former friends and allies would soon turn on him, as he became the culprit of blame for the Bonapartists and the symbol of betrayal and hatred for the royalists. The mythos of Napoleon's invincibility was still strong, and once the magnitude of the defeat became clear, a scapegoat would be needed to take the fall. With a clear understanding of the growing political situation, the marshal knew his time of influence was short.

"I have here a message from the emperor," spoke the Minister of War, Louis-Nicolas Davout. "He states that despite the setback of the northern campaign, the defence of France is paramount and ultimate victory still to be had. He notes that he defeated the Prussians at Ligny and Wavre, fought Wellington to a standstill at Quatre Bras with his only defeat coming at Waterloo. And, even then, it was the weather and terrain that decided the battle, not the tactical prowess of Wellington or Blucher. He assures us the British and Prussians are exhausted, low on resources, with crippling losses of their own to contend with. The emperor will arrive this afternoon to assure the Chambers of his certainty of success. The Russians and Austrians have been stopped and, even now, Marshal Grouchy is reforming the Armee du Nord, with regiments rallying around the stalwart Old Guard…"

"This report is false, false on all points!" Ney protested loudly, interrupting the minister. He then stepped down onto the main floor.

"Marshal Ney, you are out of order!" Davout rebuked.

"Let him speak," Marshal Soult spoke up. "He was the last to leave the field and has a perspective of the Armee du Nord's disposition that the rest of us do not."

"Very well," the minister conceded. He nodded to Ney. "Proceed."

"Grouchy cannot have under his command more than twenty thousand men," Ney observed. "There is no more than one soldier of the Imperial Guard to rally. I know, I commanded it! I saw it completely massacred before leaving the battlefield. The enemy is at Nivelle with eighty thousand men. He can be in Paris in six days. You have no way of saving the nation but to open negotiations, lest the English and the Prussian barbarians burn our beloved city to the ground."

While there was a measure of fear regarding the triumphant Wellington and his Anglo-Allied Army, the thought of the Prussians in Paris absolutely terrified the people. The English may have been centuries-old enemies of France, but at least Wellington was a gentleman. Marshal Blucher and the Prussians, on the other hand, were regarded as unwashed barbarians, no different than the Germanic hordes that battled the Roman legions two thousand years before. Whether the reputation was borne of truth or embellishment, the people of Paris were petrified at the thought of their beloved city being sacked by these rampaging savages.

The state of Napoleon's army was even more dire than Ney had stated, for in the coming days Grouchy would prove able to rally only ten thousand survivors from the Armee du Nord to defend Paris. Ney did go on to explain that even if the British and Prussians were hampered by their own losses and lack of ammunition, this would sort itself in a matter of days.

"Their wounded are already on their way back to Brussels," he said. "And no doubt their supply lines are ferrying rations and ammunition to the survivors while they march towards Paris. Even if every last man Grouchy has rallied were a member of the Old Guard, no ten thousand men can defend the city against the coming onslaught. Paris is not a fortress, and we should not let vanity and personal pride blind us to the realities of the situation."

Davout's downcast expression and lack of conviction in the report he read told the Chamber of Peers all they needed to know. Still, there were those who were not so ready to accept defeat. One of these was Charles de Flahaut, who had commanded a brigade at Waterloo and only returned the previous evening.

"The revolution cannot be undone by one setback," he said, rising to his feet. "I, too, was at Waterloo…"

"Then you should understand the devastation the army suffered," Ney interrupted. "That is, unless you were among those to first flee from the field." He had not meant to give such a biting insult towards a man he respected as a soldier, and Flahaut was clearly hurt by his words. However, he said no more and took his seat.

There was much muttering and hundreds of private conversations as the members of the Chambers talked quickly amongst themselves as to what should be done. If Marshal Ney's assessment was correct, and they had no reason to doubt him, then the war truly was lost. Ney's meeting with the Chamber of Peers would give Napoleon one more reason, however delusional, to forever hate the very man he called the 'bravest of the brave', and whom he had loved like a brother.

One man who watched the proceedings with interest was the former Minister of Foreign Affairs, Charles Maurice, also known as Prince de Talleyrand. It was no secret that Flahaut was Talleyrand's illegitimate son, though he said nothing during the young man's rather brief debate with Marshal Ney. A cold and calculating person of terrifying intelligence, he had managed to play both royalist and revolutionary over the years. Though he had turned on Napoleon in 1807, the emperor still offered him a cabinet position in his temporarily restored government upon his return from exile back in March. With a second fall likely to happen soon, Talleyrand was thankful that he was still in the good graces of King Louis and the Bourbons. The man who now argued with his son, once universally hailed as the bravest soldier to have ever lived, would be the perfect focus for the renewed wrath of the royalists.

Still, Talleyrand did, in his own way, view Michel Ney as a friend. He also knew that the marshal, while legendary as a soldier, was also very stubborn and out of his element when it came to the political realities of their fast-changing world. Whispers amongst royalist friends told Talleyrand that he was likely to become both interim prime minister and minister of foreign affairs again, once Napoleon was deposed. Ney would likely prove to be his own worst enemy in the coming months and, if possible, Talleyrand wanted to try and help the marshal from essentially hanging himself. Of course, how much influence he could exert to try and protect his friend would be dependent on the royalists' demeanour towards him, as well as the disposition of King Louis, once he returned to power. The king would likely show at least some temperance towards Napoleon's marshals and generals, yet Ney had personally betrayed him. After all, it was he who promised to bring Bonaparte back to Paris 'in an iron cage', only to abandon his king at first sight of the emperor.

Charles Maurice de Talleyrand

# Chapter V: The Betrayal of Friends

Paris, France
27 July 1815

Marshal Ney's oldest sons, Michel Louis Felix, Eugene Michel, and Joseph Napoleon
Not pictured: Edgar Napoleon Henry

For Marshal Ney, the return to Paris was bittersweet and, after his address to the Chamber of Peers, it was almost cloaked in secrecy. Napoleon's pleas to the Chambers had fallen upon deaf ears, and he was forced to abdicate once more. With Prussian cavalry fast closing on Paris, and British redcoats only a few days behind, Napoleon had fled the city. The British would likely exile or imprison him, whereas it was equally probable the Prussians would hang or guillotine him on the spot. As such, it was rumoured that Napoleon would attempt to escape from France altogether, while trying to find asylum in America.

King Louis had promptly returned to France, arriving first at Cambrai, where he proclaimed that all who had served with Napoleon during what was known as 'The Hundred Days' would not be persecuted, with the exception of 'the instigators'. This last term was quite vague and no one knew exactly who would be deemed an instigator in Napoleon's temporary return to power. On 29 June, five members of the Chamber of Peers approached the Duke of Wellington about the possibility of installing a foreign prince on the throne of France. Wellington rejected this, stating the restoration of the Bourbons was the surest way of preserving the integrity of France. Whether the Chambers had been sincere, or whether the whole display had been little more than a spectacle to show that Louis had the support of Britain, was anyone's guess.

The king arrived in Paris on the evening of 8 July to a boisterous reception, with the Tuileries Palace gardens thronged with crowds of supporters. King Louis may have been a feeble, corpulent, ass, but at least he was mostly harmless. Emperor Napoleon had been truly loved by the people, yet his defeat, along with the death and maiming of tens-of-thousands of French soldiers in the aftermath of his return, had been the death knell for the Bonapartists. Napoleon was still on the run, though he would be captured by the British Royal Navy a few days later while attempting to escape via the port at Rochefort.

Michel Ney, along with the other marshals and generals who had served under Napoleon, were left in a state of virtual limbo following the king's return. Foreign troops now occupied France once more, the French nobility was in a state of political turmoil as they sought to best placate the king and the royalists, while also trying to sort out exactly who the 'instigators' were.

It was one of the last evenings of July as Ney and his wife sat quietly down to dinner, when a loud banging was heard on the front door. Without waiting for a word, Ney's oldest son, twelve-year old Joseph Napoleon, ran to the window.

"Papa, it's the minister of police!" the lad said excitedly.

"Fouche," Aglae said quietly. "What does he want?" Her face betrayed the intense fear she held for her husband's safety. The weeks since the king's restoration had been as great a strain on her as they were on Michel. She had hoped to compel him to leave France, though he would have none of it, saying that he would not run like a coward.

"It's alright," Ney said calmly. He then nodded to his butler, "Show him in."

Ten years older than Ney, Joseph Fouche, *Duc d'Otrante*, was one of the most cunning and coldly calculating men the marshal had ever known. His tactics in supressing rebellions against Napoleon during the French Empire were both ruthless and terrifying. He was also a master of political manipulation, and had managed to maintain his posting, or at least ones very similar, under both the Bourbons and Bonaparte. It was even rumoured that the emperor had been terrified of him. How men like he and Talleyrand had managed to successfully play both sides never ceased to baffle Ney. Fouche's very appearance made Aglae shiver. Not wishing to see the minister, she quickly left the room under the guise of ushering away the children.

The door was opened and the minister of police strode in. He was plainly dressed in a great frockcoat with a black round hat, which he promptly removed. He had come alone, which at least meant he was not there to arrest Michel. And yet, the fact that he felt confident enough to travel about Paris alone at night added to his fearful mystique.

"Marshal," he said, with a respectful nod.

"Working your way back into Louis' favour, now that he's restored once more?" Ney asked plainly.

"My dear marshal, I have been in the service of *France* for over twenty years," Fouche stated. "However, I do have to look out for my own interests, as well as those who rule over us. I thought at one time to perhaps establish a republic in France, but that is now an impossibility. What does it matter to me if it's Napoleon or Louis on the throne?"

"What do you want?" Aglae said, entering the room once more, her arms folded across her chest sternly.

"Madame," the minister answered with a bow. "I am here to help your husband."

"And why would you of all people wish to help him?" she replied coldly. "You've never cared about saving anyone's life but your own."

"True," Fouche confessed with a coy grin. He stared at Ney as he continued, "But whatever you or your husband may think of me, I have always considered him a friend. I respect you, Michel.

Napoleon was right to call you the *bravest of the brave*. However, he is gone now, you must know that. His health was poor when he returned, and after what happened at Waterloo, you know he will never rise again."

"I am aware of what happened at Waterloo," Ney said calmly, with ice in his voice.

"I meant no disrespect," Fouche replied. He then produced a bound document which he handed to Ney. "Here is a passport that will allow you unhindered access out of France. Though the king is undecided as to what he should do, the ultra-royalists want you dead, Michel. You should know that you don't have many friends left amongst the Bonapartists, either. Believe me when I say you need to leave France at once."

"I am not one to run away, Joseph," Ney replied, glancing through the documents.

"It would only be for a short time," Fouche persisted. "Head to Switzerland. It is a neutral country, you will be safe there. Or perhaps you should seek passage to the United States. After all, that was Napoleon's intent, before he ran afoul of the British Royal Navy."

Both Ney and his wife's eyes grew wide at this latest statement.

Fouche simply smiled. "Of course," he said, "I forgot that not everyone receives their news as quickly as I do. Twelve days ago, while seeking to depart France near Rochefort, Bonaparte's efforts at seeking asylum in America were thwarted by a British warship, the HMS Bellerophon, if I recall. His fate is now left to the English. Still, better them than the Prussians. If those Cossacks had caught him, he'd be returned to Paris in pieces."

There was an awkward silence, though Fouche appeared to be almost smiling. It was a perverse contradiction, that he who seemed to revel in watching Ney's sense of dejection was also the very man who was offering him a passport that could save him from the king's vengeance. What Fouche did not disclose was that it was Talleyrand, as well as Ney's few remaining friends, who had attained the passport. The minister of police was only the deliverer, trying to show magnanimity under the guise of friendship. In truth, he cared nothing for what happened to Michel Ney, or any of the other marshals of Napoleon for that matter.

"Do what is right for both you and your family," Fouche persisted. "The Bonapartists are finished; there is nothing more you can do for France."

Joseph Fouche, Duc d'Otrante

Ney departed Paris with his family soon after Fouche's visit. It was assumed he was headed to Switzerland, as the minister of police had suggested. Two days later, Fouche was summoned to a personal meeting with the king, along with Talleyrand who, as predicted, was now prime minister. Other prominent nobles were also present. Among these was the powerful Duke of Richelieu, who as a lifelong royalist had served as a major general in the Russian army during the Napoleonic Wars, in his efforts to defeat Bonaparte and restore his king.

"Fouche, my friend," the king said, gesturing for the minister to take his place at the table where a blank piece of parchment and a writing quill sat. "With that little wretch, Bonaparte, at last out of our affairs, we now have a rather delicate matter we need to resolve before we can begin the long healing process for our beloved France."

"I am at your majesty's service," Fouche said with a bow, as he took his seat.

"Good," Louis grinned. "Good. I gave my word that those who fought beside the pretender during the Hundred Days would not be prosecuted, provided they were not instigators to the hated affair. I intend to keep my word on this. However, I need to know exactly who the real traitors are."

"Which is where you come in," Richelieu added. "Having been in close proximity to Bonaparte's regime, you are in the perfect position to know exactly who among the marshals and peers sought to betray our king."

Fouche did not speak, but simply took the writing quill and began to scribble names as quickly as he could. Both King Louis and the Duke of Richelieu knew Fouche's mind all too well, He would give them the most thorough list of traitors with which they could exact their vengeance. After several minutes, the minister of police slid the list across the table. While the king sat grinning with his head resting on his propped up hands, Richelieu proceeded to read some of the names.

"Emmanuel de Grouchy, Nicolas Jean-de-Dieu Soult, Jean-Baptiste Drouet, Comte d'Erlon, Jean-Baptiste Girard…"

"Girard is dead," Talleyrand interrupted. "He was severely wounded at Ligny and died nearly two weeks later from his injuries."

"We can scratch him from the list," Richelieu chuckled as he drew a line through Girard's name. He then continued, "Dominique-Joseph René Vandamme, Baron Pierre Berthezène, Count Louis de Bourmont, Georges Mouton, Comte de Lobau, Pierre Claude, Comte de Pajol, Auguste Jean Ameil…" He paused before reading the last name, which Fouche had written in larger script for emphasis. "And Michel Ney."

"A thorough list," Talleyrand observed. He chose his next words carefully. "Still, I cannot help but wonder how harsh we should be to these men; after all, most have performed lifelong service to France. Soult has served in our ranks for thirty years, and Ney was hailed as the bravest soldier of them all by both friend and enemy alike…"

"Ney!" Richelieu snapped. "Ney was the greatest traitor of them all! He who swore to bring Napoleon back in a cage of iron, instead betrays his king. We even have signed declarations by him, urging French soldiers to denounce their rightful monarch and join the usurper. I hear Ney has left Paris and is bound for Zurich in Switzerland. He'd best stay there, for if he should ever return to French soil, it will only mean his death."

"Well then," Talleyrand continued, "there is a justice to render to Duke d'Otrante. At least he has not forgotten to list any of his friends on this black list."

# Chapter VI: The Marshal's Sword

Château de Bessonies
Bessonies, France
29 July 1815

Château de Bessonies

Marshal Ney may have left Paris, but he was not headed to Zurich in Switzerland. Instead, he and his family headed south, to the Château de Bessonies in Lot. Aglae's cousin, Martine, lived there with her husband and family. Though more than three hundred miles south of Paris, Ney, along with his wife and sons, made excellent time travelling by fast coach. It was almost nightfall on 29 July when they arrived in Bessonies. Martine's husband, Ambert, was there to greet them at the chateau. A former cavalry sergeant who had been gravely wounded during the same action which saw the death of Ney's close friend, Marshal Jean-Baptiste Bessières, Ambert had been medically discharged from the army. He now walked with the aid of a cane. Although, by his own admission, he was lucky that he could stand at all. He was also a staunch Bonapartist who was unabashed in his hatred for the Bourbons.

"Dearest cousin," he said, taking Aglae's hands in his and kissing her on both cheeks. "Martine will be anxious to see you."

"Ambert, it is good to see you," Aglae replied, her voice tired.

"And you are most welcome here, Marshal of France," Ambert said as he clasped Ney's hand. "Here we honour heroes who have fought for our people, the Bourbons be damned!"

Ney's four sons were extremely weary after their long ride, though they had complained little. Even the youngest, Edgar, seemed to understand the gravity of the threats to their father. Martine came out and embraced her cousin, along with the boys. She took them inside and left Ambert to discuss things with Michel.

"It's not safe for you," the chateau proprietor said bluntly. "Both the king and prime minister have denounced you, along with many of the other Marshals of the Empire."

"That doesn't surprise me," Ney remarked. "The royalists would have every last soldier who ever stood with Napoleon shot if they could get away with it."

"Strangely enough, there were a number of names missing from the list of 'instigators'," Ambert noted. "The emperor's own brothers were not listed, though they could hardly be blamed for standing with their own brother."

"Joseph, Lucien, and Jerome are harmless," Ney observed. "They have none of Napoleon's ambition or strategic genius."

"Yes, well your name has especially drawn the ire of the royalists," Ambert said, to which Ney snorted in reply. "I'm serious, my friend. Of all of the Marshals of the Empire, it is you they hate most of all. Just yesterday, the Prefect of Cantal gave a very public denunciation of you, specifically. Anyone who sees you is to report it to the gendarmes at once. Thankfully, the public, as well as the king's ministers, all think you've gone to Zurich. Quite frankly, that would have been a safer place for you. Still, no one expects to find you here, and you are more than welcome to remain here as my guests until this whole thing blows over. Just, please, be careful is all I ask."

If Michel Ney had a grievous fault, it was that his extreme bravery was only matched by his stubborness. While he was most certainly grateful for the hospitality and protection offered to him by Ambert and Martine, he felt like a coward for hiding from the royalists. Surely one who had fought in so many savage battles, and who had triumphed over a number of France's most bitter enemies, should not have to cower in the confines of his wife's family's chateau for fear of being caught by a bunch of spoiled whelps who had power suddenly thrust upon them. He found it indignant and, some mornings, found himself almost wishing he'd be caught. He did not have long to wait.

Over breakfast on the morning of 2 August, he had shown Ambert a splendid Egyptian sword that had been a personal gift from the emperor. With a German hilt and curved Oriental-style blade it was an impressive weapon, to say the least. It was also very distinctive, and any who knew Marshal Ney were likely familiar with the sword.

Later that morning, there was a loud knock on the front door, Michel promptly went upstairs to his quarters, yet he forgot the sword on the couch in the foyer.

Ambert's butler opened the door and in walked the local captain of the Bessonies gendarmes. He removed his hat and waited in the foyer while the butler left to find his master. The sword caught his attention, and he walked over to it, his mind racing with curiosity. He turned the weapon over in his hands and pulled the blade partially from its scabbard. He gasped once he realized who the sword belonged to.

"A magnificent piece, that," Ambert said as he limped into the foyer.

"Indeed," the captain observed. "Is this yours?"

"Good Lord, no," Ambert replied with a chuckle. He tried to remain nonchalant, yet inside he was near panic. Did the captain know whose sword that was? Though hundreds-of-thousands of such weapons were issued to French soldiers over the last few decades, it was too fine of a piece to be owned by one who had only risen to sergeant in the cavalry. "It belongs to the husband of one of my wife's friends. He must have left it here. I'll have Martine send it on after him."

"I see," the captain replied, turning the sword over in his hands again. "Whoever owns this would have to be a man of great renown." He set the weapon back on the table and smiled. The officer was good friends with the chateau owners, and the last thing Ambert wanted was to deceive him. Yet, he could not bring himself to betray the marshal. At least he had been truthful in all of his answers.

"I simply wanted to stop in and say 'good morning'," the captain continued, seemingly forgetting about the sword.

At least Ambert hoped that was the case.

"My wife mentioned to me only this morning that we have not seen you in some time and asks if you and the lovely Martine would care to join us for dinner sometime this week?"

"We would be delighted," Ambert replied. "However, Martine is a bit under the weather, and we do have a couple of family guests staying with us at the moment."

"Any family of yours is welcome in my house," the captain assured him. "But please, do not trouble yourselves until after Martine is feeling well enough. And now I must bid you good day." He donned his hat, which he then touched the bill of, before leaving the chateau.

Marshal Ney's Egyptian sword, given to him by Napoleon following the Battle of Hohenlinden on 3 December 1800

Aglae was absolutely terrified when she heard about the captain's visit. Ambert assured her he had only come by to invite him and Martine to supper, and that they were good friends. He also did not enquire any more about the sword once Ambert had explained that it belonged to a family friend and he would have it sent on.

Madame Ney's fears came to fruition the following morning, when Michel opened the shutters to their bedroom window and saw that the house was surrounded by gendarmes.

"Oh my God," Aglae gasped, placing a hand over her mouth in horror.

"Easy, my love," Michel soothed her. "It is dark in this room and they cannot have seen my face." He then called out the window, *"Who is it that you want?"*

*"We are here for Marshal Ney!"* the captain of the gendarmes replied.

Ney simply nodded.

"Michel, please," Aglae pleaded, grabbing him by the arm.

"It is too late, dearest," he replied. "They know I am here. And besides, it was foolish for me to have run." He then called out the window, "Wait a moment, and I will show him to you!"

Giving his wife a gentle kiss, he left the room and walked calmly down the stairs. The captain was waiting for him in the foyer, along with half a dozen of his men. Ambert and Martine heard the commotion and were shocked at what they saw.

"I'm sorry, Ambert," the captain said sadly. He then addressed Ney. "Michel Ney, you are hearby under arrest on the charges of high treason, by order of his majesty, King Louis XVIII."

"And I will answer these charges in the courts of Paris," Ney replied, his voice still calm. "I give you my solemn word, as a Marshal and Peer of France, that I will not attempt to escape."

"Very well," the captain acknowledged. "You will not be bound, nor will you have but six of my men accompany you to Paris. At which time you will turn yourself over to the Minister of Police."

"I understand," Ney replied. He then turned to Aglae, kissing her gently, though not saying another word.

His wife held her stoic resolve until after he stepped out the front door, at which time she burst into tears, collapsing into the arms of her cousin.

It would take nearly two weeks for the marshal and his small escort to make their way back to Paris. They stopped at the nearest inn each night, where curious onlookers would gather to see the famous marshal. The gendarmes spent most of their time keeping the crowds away, and since Ney had given his word as a marshal and peer, he was neither bound nor locked away each night.

On the seventh day of their journey, a man wearing the uniform of a French general rode up to the inn where they were staying, near Bourges. The two guards outside the entrance immediately came to attention, one of them taking the general's horse as he dismounted.

"I am here to see Marshal Ney," he said, removing his gloves and hat, which he handed to the other gendarme.

"Or course, sir," the man replied. "His room is upstairs, last one on the right.

The general's name was Rémi Joseph Isidore Exelmans. Named a Peer of France soon after Napoleon's return, he had led the II Cavalry Corps at both Ligny and Wavre. And in a last-ditch effort to defend Paris, his troops had won a decisive victory over the Prussian hussars at the Battle of Rocquencourt on 1 July. Though the war was lost, thanks to Exelmans, the final battle of the Napoleonic Wars was a French victory.

Général de Division Rémi Joseph Isidore Exelmans

The pounding on the door startled Ney, but as he opened it and saw who was waiting on the other side, he smiled appreciatively.

"Rémi," he said, extending his hand, which his fellow marshal accepted warmly. "What pleasure is this? Last I heard, you were hunting Prussian Cossacks and daring them to attack Paris!"

"I couldn't let our enemies get the last word in, now could I?" Exelmans replied with a shrug. "And strangely enough, I did not end up on Fouche's list of traitors. Perhaps they figured that since they already court-martialled me once during the First Restoration and failed to get a conviction, there was no point in trying again. I have, therefore, resolved to be as much of a thorn in the side of the royalists as I can."

"Good man," Ney grinned, motioning for his friend to come in.

Exelmans looked over his shoulder before closing the door behind him, his face now deadly serious. "Listen, Michel, I am here to help you."

"Help me?" Ney asked. "How?"

"You don't have to return to Paris," Rémi emphasized. "Napoleon may be gone, but there are still plenty of men out there, men who are loyal to you. Just give the word, and I can bring a hundred cuirassiers to your aid. They'll chop these few gendarmes to ribbons, have it blamed on a band of robbers, and then we can spirit both you and your family to Zurich, all nice and clean. The king cannot touch you there. The Treaty of Paris has all of Europe in agreeance with Switzerland's eternal state of neutrality. Please, Michel, just give the word!"

"That I cannot," Ney replied, sadly shaking his head. "I gave my solemn word; my bond as both a Peer and Marshal of France. If I betray that, then the Bourbons are, indeed, justified to call for my downfall."

"Know this," Exelmans said, as he nodded his head in resignation. "It is not just exile they will seek for you. There are many among the ultra-royalists who are rather vehemently calling for your death."

"And going to Zurich will not change that," Ney replied. "No, the Duke of Elchingen will not run from his enemies. He will make his stand before his accusers."

# Chapter VII: Who Shall Judge Him?

Paris, France
19 August 1815

Marie Therese, Duchesse d'Angouleme

Marshal Ney and his escort arrived in Paris without further incident, where he was promptly imprisoned at the Conciergerie. The day they arrived, a general named Charles-Angelique Huchet, who had served as Napoleon's aide-de-camp, was executed by firing squad. This set an ominous tone for the returning marshal as he awaited his eventual fate.

Of all of Ney's most ardent haters, perhaps none lusted for his blood more than Marie Therese, Duchesse d'Angouleme, who was more commonly known as 'Madame Royale'. The only surviving child of King Louis XVI, she had seen both her father, as well as her mother, Queen Marie Antoinette, guillotined. Her brother, known officially as Louis XVII, even though he never actually attained the throne of France, died in prison. Returning to France after the First Restoration, she remained in Bordeaux upon Napoleon's return, even as the rest of the Bourbons fled the country once more. Attempting to rally troops to the royalist cause, the soldiers agreed to protect her, yet they refused to engage in civil war with Napoleon's army. She had then agreed to leave in order to save Bordeaux from senseless destruction. Despite being one of his most hardened enemies, the emperor respected her, going so far as to call her, "The only man in her family." It came as no surprise that she most vehemently of all the royalists wanted Ney dead.

Madame Royale was a witness to her uncle, the king's emergency meeting of his council, in order to decide what was to be done about Marshal Ney. The Prince de Talleyrand, who was still acting as prime minister, was present, along with the Duke of Richelieu, Joseph Fouche, the Duke of Otrante, and a host of other prominent ministers.

"Due to the marshal's bull-headed refusal to leave France, we are now in a delicate position," Fouche explained. "Had he gone to Zurich, it would have been a simple matter to sentence him to death 'in absentia', without having to go through what will now be a very public trial."

"Ney still remains popular among much of the senior officer corps, despite Bonaparte renouncing him," Talleyrand added. "It may prove difficult in finding one with sufficient rank who is willing to oversee his court-martial."

"If the Marshals of France wish to maintain their positions as such, then they will do their duty to France!" the king snapped. He then thought for a moment. "Have Marshal de Moncey preside. He owes both his marshal's baton, as well as his peerage as Baron of Conegliano, to us."

"A sound choice, sire," Fouche added. "Jeannot de Moncey was created a peer just last year, and he wisely remained neutral during the usurper's return. Gratitude and a desire to remain in your majesty's good graces should compel him to try and condemn the traitor."

Marie Therese watched the meeting in silence, though her face was red and her knuckles white as they clutched her chair. She had delighted in the death of General Hutchet, as well as the news that another abominable traitor, Grand Admiral Joachim-Napoléon Murat, had met his end. The brother-in-law to Napoleon, whom the emperor had installed as King of Naples, had tried to reclaim his throne, only to be captured by the forces of the current king, Ferdinand IV, who had the lapdog of Bonaparte executed by firing squad.

"And now the greatest traitor of them all will meet his ignominious demise," she hissed as the meeting with the ministers broke up.

"My dear Madame Royale," King Louis said, as he pulled his rotund mass from his chair. He walked over to her, and as she stood he placed a hand under her chin. "It is good you wish to see justice done for our family. We should be careful, though, that *justice* does not turn into *revenge*."

"Forgive me, uncle," the young woman replied, "but for me they are often one and the same. I never trusted the Bonapartists, especially after the brutal way in which my parents and brother were murdered. Ney's betrayal of you confirms my worst feelings about the followers of Napoleon."

"Michel Ney is indeed a traitor," Louis concurred, "and for that he must face justice. I must confess that a large part of me wishes to spare him the death sentence, and not just because of the political fallout it will bring." As he started to turn away, his niece was ever persistent.

"And what fallout could there be?" she asked. The king turned back towards her.

"The Duke of Wellington is being rather emphatic that we show a degree of clemency to the marshals and generals of Napoleon's 'empire'," he explained. "I have already stated that we would welcome back in good faith all except those who instigated the usurper's return. And while Marshal Ney is without a doubt one of these said instigators, I suspect that Wellington has a certain level of admiration, almost affection, for him."

"Wellington be damned!" Marie spat. "And all the English! Where were they when our family, and those loyal to the rightful monarchy, were being murdered in the streets of Paris? They only fought against Bonaparte when it suited them; when they finally felt threatened by his power. Opportunists, the lot of them, and they dare to tell us how to dispense justice amongst those who betrayed us?"

It was a rather precarious position for the king. The ultra-royalists were calling for Ney's blood just as vehemently as his niece, yet the moderates would push for clemency, or at least a reduced sentence. The marshal's guilt was unquestioned, it was what should be done about it. King Louis knew that Wellington was pushing for a clause within the pending treaty to end the Napoleonic Wars that would spare all of Bonaparte's former supporters from the death penalty. If Marshal Ney was to pay for his crimes with his life, then the court-martial had to move rather expediently.

Ney's 'prison' was little more than an attic room; one that he could likely escape from, if he so desired. And yet he was determined to have his day in court, where he would make his stand against those who accused him of high treason against France. Two weeks into his stay, he was paid a visit by General Exelmans, who carried a folded letter in his hands.

"The king," he said, "has ordered Marshal de Moncey to preside over your court-martial."

"Ah, our old friend and your former companion from the Battle of Valencia," Ney observed.

"Yes, well I never did fault him for my capture. The populace had risen up against us and we were simply overwhelmed. Still, my three years as a prisoner in England could have been much worse. I could be stuck in an attic awaiting trial by my own comrades." Both men shared a dark chuckle at this last remark.

"Finally," Ney replied. "I was growing tired of being forced to wait on the king's ministers to make up their minds."

"Well, you may have to wait a little longer," Rémi replied, handing him the envelope. "De Moncey may have remained neutral during the Hundred Days, but he is no traitor to his friends."

Puzzled, Ney opened the envelope and read the letter within. It was a copy of one sent to the king by de Moncey:

*I believe, that after my letter of yesterday to the Minister of War, he would have judged sufficient the reason which I gave for refusing to sit in a court martial where I could not preside. I find myself mistaken, as he has transmitted me a positive order from Your Majesty on this subject.*

*Placed in the cruel dilemma of offending Your Majesty or of disobeying the dictate of my conscience, it becomes my duty to explain myself to Your Majesty. I enter not into the enquiry whether Marshal Ney is guilty or innocence.*

*Shall 25 years of my glorious labours be sullied in a single day? Shall my locks, bleached under the helmet, be only proofs of my shame? No, Sire! It shall not be said that the elder of the marshals of France contributed to the misfortunes of his country. My life, my fortune, all that I possess or enjoy is at the service of my king and country; but my honour is exclusively my own, and no human power can ravish it from me. If my name is to be the only heritage left to my children, at least let it not be disgraced.*

*Bon-Adrien Jeannot de Moncey, Duke of Conegliano*
*Marshal of France*

"I cannot imagine the king took this too kindly," Ney remarked as he finished reading.

"That he did not," Exelmans concurred. "Louis stripped de Moncey of his marshal's baton and sentenced him to three months in prison."

"I'll be damned," Michel said, shaking his head. "Do none of my peers have the courage to stand up and judge me for my actions, lest by doing so they only incite their own guilty consciences?"

In the end, it seemed as if no one within the military wished to take part in the trial and court martial of Marshal Michel Ney. Despite wishing to remain in the king's good graces, many of France's senior generals and marshals had simply refused to take part in the proceedings.

Nearly three months would pass before both the king and his ministers were able to bring forth the council that would try Marshal Ney. Finally, Marshal Jean-Baptiste Jourdan agreed to heed King

Louis' directive to form a court-martial board. The following notice was soon posted:

*The court martial charged with the trial of Marshal Ney will meet tomorrow in the great Hall of Assize, at the Palace of Justice. It will consist of:*
*Marshal Count Jourdan, President;*
*Marshal Massena, Prince of Essling;*
*Marshal Augereau, Duke of Castiglione;*
*Marshal Mortier, Duke of Treviso;*
*Lt-General Count Villatte;*
*Lt-general Count Claparede;*
*Lt-General Count Maison, Governor of Paris.*
*Baron Joinville, Commissary Ordonnateur of the First Military Division, will perform the functions of King's Commissary, Count Grundler, Marechal de Camp, those of Judge Advocate And M. Bondion, those of Greffier.*

"I don't like this," Ney said to Exelmans, as well as his counsel. "I have long considered Massena a friend, and Jourdan I've always had immense respect for. Every last one of these men knows me, and I doubt that any of them would think me guilty of betraying my country."

"Then what's not to like?" his counsel asked, his brow furrowed in puzzlement.

"I've fought beside all of these men," Ney explained. "I've also had some rather bitter disputes with some, namely Jourdan and Massena, in Portugal."

"That was years ago," Exelmans observed. "Surely any differences you've had with them cannot still be carried as grudges!"

"I would like to think so," Ney replied. "But there is also going to be tremendous pressure coming down on them from the king. That, along with any long-term resentments any may still hold…well, let's just say, I don't like my chances with this court-martial."

"What then?" his counsel asked.

"Am I not a Peer of France, as well as one of her Marshals? Let the Chamber of Peers try me. After all, their jurisdiction rates above that of a military tribunal."

"Are you sure that's wise?" Rémi asked. "Yes, you have many colleagues amongst the Peers, but a number of them were given their peerage by the king, not Napoleon. And there are also plenty among the royalists who will influence any verdict they may reach."

"Let my peers judge me," Ney emphasized. "And let them bear responsibility for whether or not justice is meted out."

There was an air of unease throughout the tribunal hall. Clearly, neither Jourdan nor any of those seated on the benches wished to be there. This was an uncomfortable position for them to be in, yet they resolutely proceeded with opening statements.

"If it pleases your excellencies," Ney's counsel said, holding up the letter they had penned the night before. "The very competency of this court, as well as the legality of military officers trying a Peer of France, is tenuous at best. I shall read to you now the formal request, and reasons behind, Marshal Ney's request that this trial be moved from a military tribunal to the jurisdiction of the Chamber of Peers.

"Proceed," Jourdan nodded.

The counsellor then began to read:

*Although the Marshal would be anxious to justify himself, in order to be restored without reproach to his afflicted family, he refuses to acknowledge the jurisdiction of this Council. What is the motive of this temporising? Could he find elsewhere more just appreciation of his political and military conduct? He would wish to be tried by his brave comrades in arms, if he was not convinced of your incompetence.*

*The Advocate here divided his discussion into three parts:*
*1. That crimes of high treason ought to be tried by the Chamber of Peers, by the terms of the 33rd Article of the Charter.*

*2. Peers of France can only be tried criminally by the Chamber of Peers. The same holds good with respect to Marshals and Grand Officers of the Crown, who are not essentially part of the Army.*

*3. The composition of the Tribunal is not legal, even on the supposition that a Marshal is subject to military trial, for Marshals bear no analogy to Commanders-in-Chief, who may be tried by officers of the same rank.*

An uneasy silence followed as the members of the tribunal tried to ascertain the implications of Ney's request. It was Count Grundler, the King's Judge Advocate, who then spoke up.

"The country mourns this day to see placed in the ranks of the accused, one of its hitherto most glorious defenders. Fatal result of our political dissension! Fatal error, which brings down the sword of justice on one who ought to have been its firmest supporter. In times of revolution, crimes are not always punished with impartiality. You will afford an illustrious example of a military tribunal deliberating calmly, in the midst of the general effervescence of passions, on the case of an unfortunate accused. The eyes of France, of all Europe, are upon us. We shall leave this assembly with untouched consciences, and without dreading the judgement of our contemporaries or of posterity."

To which Baron Joinville replied, "His Majesty's council has taken learned research on the origins of the privileges of the peerage, and on the origin and prerogatives of the Marshals of France. And in my view of the subject, the Chamber of Peers is the only tribunal that could judge criminally a Peer of France. Marshal Ney has not lost the right of being tried by his Peers, even though his peerage was accepted under Bonaparte. An accused should always be tried according to the quality which he possessed at the time of committing the offence."

While Ney and his representative seemed satisfied to hear no rebuke from the prosecution, General Massena appeared suddenly nervous. After all, why would the king's council approve such a request so willingly? And as the Judge Advocate continued, Massena was overcome by a sense of dread, that Ney had committed a serious tactical error by not allowing himself to be tried by his fellow officers, but instead by the Chamber of Peers.

"I must point out the absurdity which might follow," Count Grundler continued, "if the sentence of this court—its competence being allowed—should go according to the regular routine of military appeals, to be investigated before the usual but inferior court of revision, which was by law composed merely of persons of the rank of colonels and of officers lower than colonels. I must ask then, if a court composed of such dignitaries as Marshals of France should have their acts revised by such a council consisting of those who are subordinate in rank?"

Jourdan then stood and said, "I move then, that we vote upon the competency of this court, and if found non-competent, then this trial must be moved to the jurisdiction of the Chamber of Peers."

The vote was soon counted and, although how each member voted was kept secret, the final tally was 5-2 in favour of declaring the court 'non-competent'. Ney looked over at Massena, who appeared crushed. The marshal had no doubt that his one-time friend had voted to send the trial to the Chambers. And while this was what Ney wanted, he knew it was because Massena and the others did not have the stomach to stand up to the king by trying Marshal Ney and rendering a verdict of 'not guilty'. Brave men they had once been, yet now they refused, almost to a man, to follow their conscience and stand by their convictions. The trial of Michel Ney would now be in the hands of the Chamber of Peers.

# Chapter VIII: False Justice

Headquarters of the British Army of Occupation
Paris, France
19 November 1815

Marshal Andre Massena

The recusing of the military tribunal was a minor irritant to King Louis, who fully expected Ney's former friends to convict him and be done with it. He had especially hoped to earn a touch of retribution against Marshal Andre Massena, who would have been disgraced at having to convict his friend. While a number of generals and marshals like Massena were not necessarily on Fouche's 'black list' of traitors, the very fact that they fought for Napoleon during the Hundred Days compelled the king to make at least a partial example of them. As it was, the court-martial declaring itself 'non-competent' was only a minor delay with Marshal Ney's trial before the Chamber of Peers set to begin in two days.

Massena had been especially fraught with doubt ever since the recusal. Firstly, he could not fathom why Ney had asked that his trial be moved to the Chamber of Peers in the first place. And secondly, he felt himself the coward for not standing up and demanding the court-martial proceed as planned. In the very least, they could have declared the marshal 'guilty under special circumstances', as it was generally accepted that Ney had only joined Napoleon when his soldiers made it clear they would re-join the emperor, rather than bring him to Paris in chains. The argument could be made that Ney had been 'swept up in the wave of Bonaparte's charisma', like most of the army. And if the members of the tribunal had been particularly brave and willing to risk the wrath of the king and the ultra-royalists, they could very well have declared Marshal Ney 'not guilty'. Much to Andre's regret, it was now too late for any of this. He, therefore, decided that before the trial went before the Chambers, he should speak with the one person who had no personal stake in Marshal Ney's fate, yet who also wielded vast amounts of power. That man was Field Marshal Sir Arthur Wellesley, the Duke of Wellington.

As Andre made his way through the misty streets towards the Duke's headquarters, he could not help but think back to his more 'colourful' history with Wellington. The two had battled each other incessantly during the Peninsular War in Portugal and Spain. Massena's terrible defeat at the Battle of Sabugal in April 1811 had later led to his dismissal from active campaigning by Napoleon. Four years later, he now hoped that Wellington's political savvy matched his battlefield prowess.

"I fear the good marshal has made a terrible mistake," Massena lamented, after he was ushered into the Duke's parlour. A servant offered him a glass of claret, which he readily accepted. "I mean, his fellow generals would at least remember his heroic exploits. I admit, it is doubtful he would be acquitted; however, the memory of his bravery would have compelled them to show clemency. The Chamber of Peers, I fear, are loyal to the Bourbons. They will know only his crime and will condemn him for it." What Massena would not say is whether or not he had voted for recusal. Either he voted against it and was angry at his peers for failing to stick to their convictions, or his own resolve had failed him and he was now filled with regret. It mattered not to the Duke.

"The treaty I am working to finish with his majesty's government expressly forbids the use of capital punishment against Napoleon's former generals," Wellington explained. "There have been no objections made to this provision, therefore, once it is signed Marshal Ney cannot *legally* be sentenced to death."

"When do you expect this to be finished?" Massena asked.

"Tomorrow," the Duke replied. "There are six separate conventions that had to be accomplished; articles on the slave trade, pecuniary indemnity, convention of military line to include articles on deserters, as well as tariffs on provisions and hospitals, private claims against France, claims of British subjects, and the Act of Neutrality of Switzerland. But not to worry, by letter of the law at least, your friend will be safe from the firing squad."

"I hope so," Massena replied, finishing his claret in one nervous gulp.

Another former officer of Napoleon had already had the sentence of death handed down to him, given he was neither a marshal, nor even French for that matter, little attention was given to his fate. The man's name was John-Jacob Lehmanowski. A colonel of Polish lancers, he was also the former chief-of-staff for Marshal Ney who had served with him both in Russia and Belgium. During the British advance at the end of the Battle of Waterloo he had been wounded in the leg and subsequently captured. That he was paroled back to the French had been his downfall, for they elected to try him for treason and make an example out of him.

His prison was little more than a room on the uppermost floor of an old chateau that looked down upon a river. Two other Polish soldiers shared the 'cell' with him, which was actually quite comfortable in both furnishings and bedding.

"Only trouble is we have to bang on the door and get one of the guards to escort us whenever we have to piss or shit," one of the men grumbled.

"Still, I could stay here indefinitely, if not for the fact our former allies now wish to hang or shoot us," the other observed. He then looked over at Lehmanowski. "What say you, colonel?"

"You two may get off with a short prison sentence," Jacob replied, "but they've already decided to send me back to Poland riddled with holes. Well, I'll have none of it. To hell with King Louis and his sense of false justice!" He stood up from the bed and gazed out the window. "How far down do you suppose it is to the river?"

"I'd say sixty or so feet," one of the men conjectured. "You've got the side of the chateau, plus the rocky cliffs that lead down to the water's edge. What are you thinking then, sir?"

The colonel gave a short laugh and opened the trunk near the bed. "Our gracious hosts determined that as an officer I was allowed to keep part of my baggage with me," he said, pulling out an assortment of shirts and trousers. "It's no more than thirty feet down the side of the wall. If need be, I'll jump the remaining thirty to fifty feet down into the river. It's fairly deep with only a modest current. Come, help me start tying all of these garments together. There is enough here, along with the bedding and sheets, to give us more than enough for a rope."

"What I can't believe is the French are so damned careless!" one of the soldiers remarked.

"We're nobodies to them," Jacob stated. "I doubt anyone will even care that we slipped away."

It took them the better part of an hour, with Jacob checking and rechecking every knot and making certain that neither garment nor bed sheet would tear.

"We'll go one at a time, just to make certain," he directed.

They then carried the bed over to the window, making sure they did not drag it and make an unnecessary racket. The Polish colonel wrapped their makeshift rope around both bedposts before tossing the remnants out the window. He looked down and, despite the dark of night, was able to see with the moonlight, as well as the glow coming from a couple of the rooms within the chateau. As it was a chilly night, it was doubtful any of the windows were left open.

He slowly lowered himself down, making certain of his footing against the rough stone. With each knot he grabbed he silently prayed they would not unravel or rip. There was a ground floor window directly below them; however, the lights were extinguished within. Still, the colonel made certain he stepped to the outside, lest unfriendly eyes catch sight of him.

Though built right up against the cliff, there was still about a two-foot ledge he was able to gain his footing on before looking around and gathering his bearings. The rock wall was far too steep for him to climb down While he was not particularly fond of heights, he was less inclined to meet the firing squad. He looked up towards the window and waved to his companions, signaling he was going to jump. One of the men nodded in acknowledgment. Jacob used the rope to help turn himself about so he could make a decent leap away from the cliffs. The last thing he wanted was to come up short and hit the rock face on the way down. He took a deep breath, held his nose while closing his eyes, and sprung from the wall as best as he was able.

The fall lasted no more than a couple seconds, yet it felt like an eternity. Jacob struggled to hold his breath in, as he wanted to give a great shout as he fell. He kept the air in his lungs, knowing it would add to his buoyancy and help him surface quicker. His feet pierced the water with a loud splash that he reckoned would wake the entire garrison at the chateau. Down, down he sank, and he thought for a moment he might actually hit the bottom of the river. The pressure was great upon his ears, and he blew hard with his nose held in order to counter this. He allowed himself to relax and started to methodically stroke his arms, pulling himself up to the surface. His lungs ached and screamed for air as he continued upward. Then, without warning, he splashed above the surface, blowing out hard and then gasping in relief. He began treading water and looked up at the chateau. His first companion had started his descent. Jacob turned himself about and started swimming towards the far bank. He was about halfway across when he heard the first splash, and was pulling himself onto the muddy riverbank when he heard the second.

He knelt amongst the tall reeds and watched for his friends. Had he not known what to look for, he never would have spotted them. What at first appeared to be either a round shadow or a rock was clearly moving towards him. It was another minute before he saw the second. It had been perhaps five minutes since he first started his climb out the window before all three were gathered on the far side of the river.

"Well, this has ruined my best shirt and trousers," the colonel laughed.

The excitement and blood rushing through their veins countered the effects of the cold river, although a gust of November wind quickly chilled them.

"What now, sir?" one of the men asked, slowly catching his breath.

"You two should head for home," Jacob answered. "With all you've already been through, I'm certain a short, thousand-mile trek back will be easy enough."

"I hear that Duchy of Warsaw is being reorganized back to the Kingdom of Poland," one of the men stated.

"Well, you will find out before I will," the colonel observed with a friendly slap on the shoulder. He looked back across the water and saw that all was still at the chateau. It was not even midnight yet, and it would be well after dawn by the time their absence was noted. He wondered if anyone would even bother looking for them.

"And what will you do, sir?" the second soldier asked.

"Keep an eye on an old friend," the colonel replied.

The trial of Marshal Ney began in earnest on 21 November. A much grander spectacle than the small tribunal of seven military officers, the Chamber of Peers was crammed with those nobles who would decide the marshal's fate. The Chambers had undergone some changes over the preceding few months. Twenty-nine peers had been removed, likely due to their Bonapartist sympathies, with an additional ninety-four appointed by the king in August. And, as Massena had feared, most of these were either ultra-royalists or sympathetic to their cause. Those peers appointed post-Revolution or by Napoleon who remained, while still making up a large percentage of the total body, were very reluctant to risk bringing the wrath of the king or the royalists down upon themselves.

# Chapter IX: Condemned

Paris, France
1 December 1815

Aglae Louise Auguié Ney, Duchesse d'Elchingen

The trial was proceeding quickly, with the verdict and sentencing expected within days, when Madame Aglae Ney received an unexpected visitor. She had made every effort thus far to put on a brave face in front of her sons, yet inside she was breaking. Four months had passed since her husband's arrest, and no resolution had been found as to what his fate should be. Marshal Nicolas Soult had been sent into exile, while others, such as General Charles Reille, had been pardoned by the king. Even Napoleon's brother, Jerome, who had commanded a division at Waterloo, was spared from the brunt of the royalists' wrath. He had gone into voluntary exile as well, something which Aglae now wished her husband had done.

The royalists were screaming for Michel's blood.

A loud knocking at the front door startled her and, after a few moments, the Prince de Talleyrand was ushered in. Having resigned as prime minister in September, in part over the treaty being negotiated with the Duke of Wellington, he had restricted himself to the role of 'elder statesman'. Aglae scowled at him, feeling the prince had been all too keen to see to her husband's arrest and trial for treason.

"What do you want, Talleyrand?" she asked indignantly.

The prince's fealty was questionable at best; indeed, it was impossible to know where his loyalties lay. Though holding no official capacity within the French government, he continued in his intrigues. Often criticizing, it seemed, absolutely everyone from the king to his most ardent opponents.

"To warn you, Madame," he answered plainly, "your husband has made a gross tactical error in protesting his court-martial. I will admit he was wise in refusing parole to his home city, seeing as how it is now in Prussian territory, and we both know what they would do to him. However, by insisting that he be tried in the Chambers, he has placed himself in even greater jeopardy." He paused for a moment to let Madame Ney comprehend what he was saying. "I must tell you," he continued, "despite the prohibitions laid out in the Treaty of Paris, the Chamber of Peers intends to sentence the good marshal to death."

"No," Aglae whispered, shaking her head in disbelief. "They can't do this!"

"The king can do whatever he wishes," Talleyrand replied. "The Chambers are anxious to appease him and the bloodlust of the royalists. Even most of the Bonapartists have abandoned your husband. Napoleon let it be known he blames Ney for his defeat. It brings me no joy to say this, Madame, but all are calling for the death of Michel Ney, Marshal of France."

"My husband is no traitor!" Aglae protested, tears of frustration and despair welling up in her eyes.

"It is not for me to say," the prince remarked coldly. He then said bluntly, "There is one man who can save him. And if you want your husband to have any chance at life, then you *must* seek the aid of the very man who defeated him at Waterloo."

Though some may have viewed her requesting an audience with Wellington as grovelling before one's enemy, Aglae was willing to go to any length to save her husband's life. Having concluded the Treaty of Paris, the Duke would be returning to England soon, even though he would remain as Commander-in-Chief of the British

Contingent of the Army of Occupation in France. The command of all infantry regiments now fell under the direct command of Lieutenant General Sir Rowland Hill. It was he who first greeted Aglae upon her arrival at the army's headquarters, after she was escorted in by a pair of redcoats.

"Madame Ney, vous êtes les bienvenus," he said with a respectful nod, welcoming her. Hill was of average height, slightly overweight with a florid complexion and receding hairline. Upon first sight, one would never guess he was one of Britain's most brilliant generals and, indeed, perhaps the only one who Wellington ever trusted with completely independent command. It had also been one of his regiments, the 52$^{nd}$ Oxfordshire, that flanked and thereby completed the rout of the French Imperial Guard at Waterloo; thankfully, Aglae was unaware of this.

"Je vous remercie," she replied with a nod. She then spoke in English, "I have come to see the Duke of Wellington. It is quite urgent."

Aglae had met the Duke before, during the initial period of peace before Napoleon's most recent return to power. Wellington had then been the British Ambassador to Paris, and the two had spoken at several social engagements. He had even gone hunting with her husband just a week before Bonaparte's escape from exile, when the two would then become mortal enemies once again.

"Madame Ney," the Duke said, as he took Aglae's hand and kissed it. "A pity we could not have met again under more favourable circumstances."

"It is those circumstances with which I wish to speak with you," Aglae replied.

"Indeed."

"My husband is to be condemned and sentenced to death." Aglae's direct and rather candid reply gave Wellington pause.

Judging from his demeanour, he was not completely surprised. "I see," he said. "And are you asking me to save your husband?"

"You are the only man who can," Aglae stated. "The king owes his restoration to you. And besides, the sentence of death against one of Bonaparte's former marshals goes against the Treaty of Paris."

"I'm well aware of that," the Duke replied coolly. "But you have not answered my question, Madame. Do you wish for me to try and save your husband? If you want the assistance of the Duke of Wellington, one must ask for it."

"I am not asking you," Aglae said, shaking her head. "I am begging you! Please know there is nothing I would abstain from doing if it meant saving Michel from his ignominious fate."

The Duke raised an eyebrow at this last remark. Madame Ney was, indeed, a very beautiful woman, and he suspected she was willing to give anything, including her virtue, if it would save her husband. Wellington was a notorious womanizer who was known for his extremely voracious sexual appetite; however, he was neither predator nor pursuer of emotionally weakened women. And he most certainly would never demean himself by sleeping with the wife of a man, who though recently his enemy, he respected greatly.

"Never beg," the Duke responded. "It is unbecoming of a lady of your eminence. And do not offer me anything, for there is nothing I would take from the wife of the Duke of Elchingen. Know this, I will do all I can to save the Marshal of France; not for you nor for his friends who have since played him false, and not even for France, but for simple justice. If I can save your husband from the firing squad or the gallows, it will be because it was the right thing to do, nothing more." He took her hand and kissed it once more. "Now go with the knowledge that Marshal Ney can count the Duke of Wellington as one of his friends…one who will not become like Judas to him."

Aglae left with conflicted feelings of both hope and trepidation. Wellington had most certainly not promised her anything; after all, how could he? Even the man who defeated Napoleon did not possess unlimited power. By the same token, the duke was the only man of influence who was even offering to help.

On 2 December, King Louis held a magnificent dinner party in celebration of the pending demise of the man he deemed to be France's most vulgar and despicable traitor. The magnificent hall at the palace was filled with both members of the Chamber of Peers, as well as many nobles amongst the ultra-royalists.

*"Le Duc de Wellington!"* a porter announced.

Wellington donned his scarlet frock this evening, complete with all of his numerous military decorations. He carried his bicorn hat under his arm as he strolled with purpose into the entrance hall. Gathered on either side of the throne dais were Fouche, Talleyrand, Prime Minister Richelieu, and a handful of others. While all stared at the British field marshal, with Talleyrand looking rather uncomfortable, the king himself stood in front of the throne, his back turned. The rebuke was absolute, for to turn one's back on someone was considered the most paramount insult. Most of the ministers looked down at the floor, unwilling to catch Wellington's seething glare. Only Fouche dared look at him, his smirk of defiance adding to the affront. The Duke said nothing, but very calmly turned and walked out of the hall.

"That takes care of the British," Richelieu said with a short laugh as the king turned around. His face was red, as if he could not believe the nerve he had shown to the man who, for all intents and purposes restored him to the throne of France.

"Yes," Louis replied, taking his seat upon the throne once more. "Wellington may have deposed the usurper, but I will not prostrate myself before him in supplication."

"A shame he could not stay," Madame Royale said as she walked over, waving her paper fan absently. "I hear the Duke rather enjoys a good ball."

"The sooner he is out of France the better!" Fouche muttered coldly.

Wellington left the palace in a fury. Never one to betray his emotions publicly, it took every ounce of his resolve to restrain himself after the king's abominable insult.

"Your grace," a woman's voice said quickly, stopping the Duke in his stride. His eyebrow raised at the sight of the rather fetching woman. She was tall, almost the same height as he, with dark blonde hair that was pinned up. He guessed she was in her late thirties, though age had done little to temper her beauty nor did it appear that her body had ever felt the ravages of childbirth.

"Can I help you?" he asked, removing his hat for a moment.

"It is I who can help you," the woman answered with self-assurance. "Or, rather, I think it is we together who can help a mutual friend." She presented her hand. "My name is Ida Saint-Elme."

"No, it isn't," Wellington replied as he kissed the back of her hand. Her head cocked to one side as he continued. "Your name is Maria Versfelt, although that is not a name you most commonly use. Usually it's Elzelina, or Ida in this case. You also write and are a stage actress, under the name *La Contemporaine*."

"My dear Duke," Ida replied, blushing. "You know a lot about me, I see."

"I make it my business to know about people," he replied. He folded his arms across his chest. "You were the lover of General Moreau for four years."

"Yes, well, he was a traitor but I still mourned his death," Ida remarked. "I suppose you know about my other long-term love interest?"

"Of course." The corner of Wellington's mouth turned upward slightly. "For fifteen years, I think everyone except Madame Ney knew you shared her husband's bed while he was on campaign."

"I've always had a bit of an adventurous side," Ida grinned. "I often dressed as a serving boy, and always stayed close by his side. I've sometimes wondered if his soldiers, who saw me going into his tent at night, thought their commander was a homosexual."

"If they did, their vision is severely impaired," Wellington scoffed. "During the Peninsular War, I caught sight of you a couple of times. Even at a distance, through my telescope, I could tell right away you were no man. Ney's soldiers likely knew it and kept quiet out of respect or they were all blind as bats."

"Yes, well, my purpose for finding you is to offer my assistance." The two started walking, and before Ida could continue, the Duke spoke up.

"The street is no place to continue this discussion. Meet me at my headquarters building at exactly 6:30. Do not be late."

Maria Versfelt, a.k.a. Ida Saint-Elme

# Chapter X: Son of France

Mocksville, North Carolina
May, 1828
\*\*\*

Some days Peter felt as though he would never be able to truly find peace. After his departure from Cheraw, he'd had little trouble finding employment, yet there was always the underlying fear he'd be recognized once more. America was a place of refuge for a number of French soldiers from Napoleon's former *Grande Armee* and, as such, Peter often feared being spotted. It upset him greatly, for whenever he saw an old Grenadier or Hussar, he wanted nothing more than to go up to the man and take him by the hand. But he knew he could not, for while there were a number of immigrants from the old country that would welcome the chance of meeting him, there were likely an equal number who would kill him on sight.

The previous fall, during a short trip to Raleigh, Peter had seen a group of older gentlemen with thick, bushy moustaches, and who carried themselves like soldiers. One of them pointed to him and shouted, *"Le maréchal vit! The Marshal lives!"* While he wished he could have greeted the men as friends, Peter knew he had to leave quickly, lest it create public spectacle. After that, he mostly avoided going to the larger cities. Even in a small community like Mocksville, there was always the chance of being recognized by unfriendly eyes. Still, he made sure he did his duty as schoolmaster.

It wasn't that he lacked for money, nor did he necessarily need the employment. It was that he felt an overwhelming desire to give back to this land that had given him a second chance at life. That, and the thought of living out his years as a recluse while waiting for old age to take him, did not sit well. Like he told his old friend, Benjamin Rogers, God had given him another chance at life. It would be an insult to the Almighty if he did not make good use of the added time.

And while he kept himself busy with teaching, as well as keeping relatively active in the local community, it was tempered by the near-endless mourning from the knowledge he would never see his wife and children again. He immersed himself in his work to keep his mind occupied, yet he found himself thinking of them constantly. Three of his sons were now grown men, quite possibly with sons of their own. The youngest, who he had not seen since he was three, would be fourteen by now and ready to come into his own before long.

It was a spring afternoon when Peter was recognized in the most welcome of circumstances. As he walked along the street towards his home, not far from the school, Peter saw a young man riding a horse at breakneck speed. He reined his mount in as he saw the old schoolteacher, then quickly dismounted. He was tall, almost the same height as Peter, and strongly built.

"Mister Ney?" he asked, out of breath.

Peter was wearing a top hat, spectacles, and had his collar turned up so his face was not completely visible.

"Yes?" he replied squinting, as he felt he should know this young man. "Do I know you?"

As the man tethered his horse, he swallowed hard and almost tripped over his feet. His face was red, though not from being winded. His eyes were wet with emotion as he struggled to speak. "You know me, sir," he said, his voice near breaking. "Or rather, you knew me in a past life."

Peter gasped in realization, his bag dropping to the ground.

"By God," he whispered, suddenly recognizing the face he had not seen in thirteen years, since the man who stood before him was a boy of seven. "*Eugene?*"

The young man simply nodded, unable to speak further. It was almost unheard of for the old schoolmaster to show extreme emotions, especially in public. And yet, as curious onlookers walked past, he no longer cared. He quickly removed his hat and spectacles so the young man could fully see his face, grabbing him by the shoulders before embracing him hard.

"My son!" He wept. Regaining his composure, he quickly guided the young man the short distance down the street to his residence. His hands trembled as he unlocked the door. He ushered Eugene into his study, pouring him a drink with his still-shaking hand. He only allowed himself a small amount of whiskey, lest this entire scene prove to be a mirage brought on by the effects of alcohol.

Neither man could speak for nearly thirty minutes.

Finally, Eugene found his voice. "It took me a long time to find you," he said, "months, in fact. I've been in America since February."

"But why are you here?" Peter asked. "Make no mistake, I am overjoyed to see you."

"I came to find you, father," Eugene explained. "All we heard were traces of rumours, hushed whispers. Mother believed you still lived, though she could never confirm this with any certainty. She managed to gain an audience with the Duke of Wellington only once, and he spoke very cryptically to her, neither confirming nor denying anything. He further implored her to never see him again, as it would be improper for him to wantonly associate with the widow of one executed for treason. We grew up without a father, and without a real place within the new social orders of France."

"Your mother never remarried then?" Peter asked.

"No," Eugene replied, shaking his head. "She has had no shortage of potential suitors, yet she has spurned every last one. It was last year, when I decided there was nothing left for me in France and that I needed to begin my own life in a new land, that she told me why. She never stopped believing that you survived; after all, she refused to even attend your supposed burial. She told me it would have been grossly improper, likely an offence against God Himself, were she to give herself to another while her husband, that she truly loved, still lived. She asked me to find you, that her conscience may at last know peace."

"Your mother was everything to me. I would give anything to see her, to hold her once more," Peter said, his eyes lost in thought of another, happier time. After a few moments of reminiscing he became focused once more. "And what of your brothers?"

"Joseph is now married," Eugene replied. "His wife's name is Albine Laffitte. They were wed just two weeks prior to my departure for America."

"Ah, so now I have a daughter-in-law," Peter smiled.

"Yes," Eugene replied. "And surprisingly, the king allowed him to retain the title of *Prince de la Moskowa*."

"The king," his father growled. "Good riddance to that vulgar, fat bastard." Louis XVIII, never one for robust health, had died four years prior. His brother now ruled as King Charles X.

"Yes, well none of us mourned his loss," Eugene agreed. He continued, "Michel is now a soldier, a lieutenant in the Chasseurs. And young Edgar Napoleon is fast growing into a fine young man."

"I am glad," Peter replied, reaching over and placing a firm grip on his son's hand. "In fact, I have not known this kind of joy in many years. And yet, it is mitigated by the knowledge that I will again never see those I most love. God has been very gracious in allowing me to see you once more."

"The Bourbon monarchy is not very strong," Eugene remarked. "The king has bolstered the power of the clergy and nobility, yet the masses hate him. I doubt anyone has the stomach for another revolution like we saw during the last century. However, it would not surprise me to see Charles deposed by the Chamber of Peers."

"It matters not who rules France," Peter replied. "Remember, I was called 'traitor' by both Bourbon and Bonapartist; royalist and revolutionary alike damned my name. There are those who once called me 'friend' who would be just as anxious to see me dead as those most loyal to the Bourbons. If it is ever revealed that I live, my enemies will make certain to enforce the sentence the Chambers passed on me all those years ago. It would also make life unsafe for your mother and brothers. No, my son, I can never return home."

"I will write to Mother," Eugene promised. "She needs to know her hope has not been in vain all these years."

"Yes," his father replied with a nod. "But not under your name. I was foolish to have allowed my pride to make me keep my family name. If you are to remain in America and truly start life anew, then you must abandon the name of Ney."

"Perhaps," Eugene replied, "but I will not do so completely. I will assume the surname of *Neyman*. Like you, I will not completely abandon my heritage. You'll also be pleased to hear that I am enrolling in the Faculty of Medicine in Baltimore."

"My boy, that is wonderful news!" Peter said enthusiastically. He was then rather sombre, as well as philosophical. "How appropriate that my son should learn to heal, whereas his father spent a lifetime killing."

The next day, father and son parted once more, both now living under assumed names. Peter Stuart Ney would continue to live as a professor in North Carolina, while his son enrolled into medical school under the name E.M.C. Neyman.

A new student had arrived in Peter's classroom. Thirteen years of age, he was the son of a riverboat captain. As such, he had never really had any place to call 'home', having travelled about extensively with his father. It was his name that brought a grin to his headmaster's face.

"Alexander Reille," he said, reading the lad's transcripts from his previous school.

"Yes, sir," the boy answered. Having heard about Mister Ney's reputation for discipline, he stood rigid at attention, his eyes fixed straight ahead.

"You bear the name of a famous general of France," Peter noted, referring to General Honoré Charles Reille, who had commanded Napoleon's II Corps at Waterloo.

"Yes, sir," Alexander replied. He added, "As do you, sir."

"I suppose I do," the schoolmaster stated. He then dismissed the lad to take his seat.

Alexander soon proved to be an astute learner, always conscious of living up to what his teacher called, "a most noble name". Given that his father had known absolutely nothing about their genealogy, the young lad tried to learn all he could about the Reilles and their impact on the history of France. Of course, there was no way of knowing if he was in any way related to General Reille, though it brought him immense pleasure to think about the possibilities. Strangely enough, when asked about his own possible relation to the famous marshal of the same surname, Peter Ney would simply gloss over or avoid the question altogether.

Though neither knew it at the time, their first meeting would have a profound impact on both of their lives in the coming years.

# Chapter XI: Shadowy Stratagems

British Army of Occupation Headquarters
Paris, France
3 December 1815

General Sir Robert Thomas Wilson

Wellington was pacing slowly in the large drawing room he was using to conduct business, before his return to England in a few weeks. It was a strange twist of fate for him, that he should now conspire against the very man who he helped restore to the throne of France, in order to save his former enemy. And yet, he was not about to let justice be so grossly perverted by that corpulent bastard who once more ruled the French. The Duke was usually very stoic, never allowing his emotions to cloud his better judgment, yet he admitted to himself that Louis' inexcusable insult towards the very man he owed his restoration to infuriated him.

Just as the hour struck 6 o'clock, there was a knock at the door.

"Come!" the Duke said, continuing to pace.

The door opened and in walked a pair of officers. They were Brevet Colonel the Honourable William Stewart, Commander of 3$^{rd}$ Battalion of the Grenadier Guards; and Lieutenant Colonel Sir

Andrew Barnard, Commander of the 1st Battalion, 95th Rifles. Barnard's green tunic with black trim contrasted sharply with Stewart's traditional British scarlet as they stood before the Duke.

"Gentlemen," Wellington said with a nod. He then looked to Stewart. "Colonel, I see you still walk with a limp. How are you managing these days, sir?"

"I manage as well as one is able, sir," Stewart replied. He had taken the brunt of an explosive carcass shot from a mortar at the Battle of Quatre Bras, two days prior to Waterloo. Thrown from his horse, with numerous shards of white-hot metal searing his flesh, he had been fortunate to have survived at all.

While Barnard had been wounded during the intense fighting around La Haye Sainte at Waterloo, he had long since fully recovered from his injuries.

"I have a rather delicate mission for both of you," Wellington explained. "A certain person of extreme importance will be departing Paris within the next few days. I will require your help in seeing to it that he makes it safely to Bordeaux."

"I have plenty of men who can provide escort," Stewart asserted.

"You will do nothing of the sort," the Duke immediately rebuked. "As I said, this is a rather delicate mission and needs to be treated as such."

"May we ask, sir, who is this person in need of our protection?" Barnard asked.

"No, you may not," Wellington replied bluntly. "Suffice it to say, this person is important to His Britannic Majesty's government, yet he is one that our current allies in France wish dead."

It was only a half-truth about Ney's importance to the British government, yet it would suffice the officers' curiosity. After all, the last thing Wellington wanted was for half of the army to be in on the plot. The only reason Wilson, Bruce, and Hutchinson knew was because he needed them to oversee the most crucial phase of the mission. He anticipated that while portraits of Marshal Ney were in existence, most of his officers and men had not studied them to the point they would know his face, should they come into close contact with him.

"Very good, sir," Barnard replied, standing rigid.

"This man will be traveling alone," Wellington continued. "You will be given a description of his appearance and what manner he will be clothed. You will then pass this on to competent subordinates, for I do not want either of you directly involved. Colonel Barnard, you have detachments of sharpshooters covering the roads between here and Orleans."

"Yes, sir."

"Their new mission is to protect this man as covertly as possible," Wellington ordered. "If he is threatened in any way, they are to shoot his assailants on sight."

"Understood. I will pass the word to one of my battalion majors, posted in Orleans."

The land was still marred by disorder following the fall of Napoleon, and so the Army of Occupation had a large amount of latitude regarding the use of lethal force. Therefore ordering Colonel Barnard's riflemen to kill any who threatened a person of importance would not arouse suspicion.

"Colonel Stewart," the Duke said. "While most of your battalion is in Orleans, you have elements spread out between there and Poitiers."

"Yes, sir," the colonel acknowledged. "Three companies under Major Webster have set up checkpoints along the road to check for suspicious persons or cargo."

"Webster," Wellington thought for a moment, then remembered the officer mentioned. The corner of his mouth twisted into almost a grin for the briefest of moments. "Yes, he will do. This will be another opportunity for him to demonstrate his worth."

The Duke gave each officer a sealed envelope. He told them to read the instructions carefully, pass his orders on to their subordinates, and then burn the messages. He checked his watch and then quickly dismissed them.

"Ten minutes," he observed, as he poured himself a glass of claret. Though the most flexible of men when it came to adjusting time and strategy on the battlefield, the duke was a stickler for promptness and efficiency. Every phase of this operation, from now until his charge was out of France, would take near-exact timing.

Soon the clock in the hall chimed 6:30, though this time there was no knock, the door was simply opened.

"Madame Versfelt," Wellington said, his back to the door, hands clasped behind him.

"I did not wish to keep your grace waiting," Ida replied. As the duke turned to face her, he noted her face was flushed, and she looked rather dishevelled. And yet, there was a gleam of hope in her eyes. She then said, "I can help smuggle our friend out of Paris, provided he survives his…execution." Clearly she hated saying the last word, and looked as if it would make her sick to say it again.

"Those responsible will be here in twenty minutes," Wellington replied. "You will be gone well before they arrive. Now, how is it you plan on getting the good marshal safely away?"

"I've spoken with Sister Therese at the maternity hospice. It has been used before as a place to keep bodies of the recently executed before internment. She feels as we do, that the sentence of death for Marshal Ney is a travesty, and she has promised to aid us in any way possible."

"And you trust her?" the Duke asked.

"I do," Ida said with a quick nod. "I have had dealings with her in the past. She is a very kind soul, one who abhors the use of capital punishment, especially for one as brave as the marshal. But first there will be the matter of the execution itself. Firstly, it will be a very public affair. And also, not only is a doctor required to verify that the condemned is, in fact, dead, but the officer commanding is obligated to first fire a last pistol shot into the executed man's head."

"And I suppose you have a stratagem to assist us with that?" Wellington had his arms folded across his chest. In truth, Maria Versfelt fascinated him. She was clearly very intelligent and had not only predicted what the Chambers' verdict and sentence would be, but had thought through a plan to save Marshal Ney from certain death.

"I have…*friends* in a few positions that will be of use," she replied with a sly grin. "They could create a stir, stating that a public execution of Marshal Ney would be bad publicity for the king, and that the matter should be settled well before the appointed hour. Add a sense of urgency to be done with it and no one is left the wiser."

Ida was smiling hopefully, though Wellington said nothing for a few moments before checking his watch yet again.

"It is time for you to leave," he said. "You will assist the good sister and ensure that our friend is spirited out of Paris. Also, know that I will play no direct hand in this affair, and will deny we ever spoke of it."

"Of course." Ida curtseyed before starting for the door. She turned and eyed the Duke with a glint in her eye. "Should I ever see you again, your grace?"

Wellington thought for a moment. "If you should request the Duke of Wellington's company, he would be remiss to deny you."

Ida smiled and curtseyed once more. It was 6:40 when she left and 6:45 when the door was knocked upon once more. A British officer in a general's uniform was ushered in.

"Sir Robert," the Duke said with a nod.

"You sent for me, your grace?" the man asked. His name was Sir Robert Thomas Wilson. During the Peninsular War he had organized a corps of Portuguese soldiers under his command, at one time preventing the French from cutting off Wellington's forces following the Battle of Talavera.

"I did," Wellington acknowledged, motioning towards a tray with a decanter of claret. This was his last meeting of the evening, and also the most important. As such, the Duke did not feel the need to rush. Sir Robert was a bit surprised there wasn't a servant in the room to offer him a glass, though he quickly surmised the nature of the duke's meeting was to be extremely private. He recalled the two soldiers outside the door who ushered him in were not privates, as one would expect to be on guard duty, but a pair of officers.

"You've no doubt heard about the actions of our new friends in the French Chambers," the duke said, taking up his own glass.

"If they do as we suspect, and push for the death penalty, it will be a despicable act that flies in the face of common decency," Wilson replied without bothering to conceal the venom in his voice. "It will also flout the Treaty of Paris, even before the ink has fully dried."

"Ironic isn't it, that we, the marshal's enemies, should wish to save him from the betrayal wrought by his own countrymen." Wellington spoke slowly, wishing to fully garner Wilson's disposition before engaging him fully with his intentions. He had little doubt that Sir Robert felt the same as he did; plus, he held the same level of loathing towards King Louis as the duke.

"He was a worthy foe," Wilson replied, "and a far better man than that walking sore, whose dynasty was only restored by the blood of British soldiers." The term *walking sore* was an insult that

Wellington had often used to describe the king, with many of his officers finding it to their liking.

"The bravest of the brave," Wellington continued. "That is what both his friends and enemies called him. During my time as Ambassador to Paris, before Boney's return, I had a few dealings with our friend. We even went hunting once. To think that in a few short months we were back to trying to butcher each other"

"And now he will be murdered by his own people," Wilson noted.

The Duke turned and looked at him. "It *is* murder, your grace." Wellington then set down his glass and paused before speaking again. "What would you say if I told you we could prevent this murder?"

"Just tell me what you need me to do, sir!" Wilson's jaw was clenched in determination.

Wellington nodded slowly. "Those two men outside the door, Bruce and Hutchinson, will assist you," he said. "Officially, you will be witnesses to the execution. Once completed, you will see to it that the 'body' is taken to a maternity hospice under the care of a Sister Therese."

"Very good, sir."

"We will also need to make assurances regarding the members of the firing squad, as well as the weapons they are issued," Wellington added. "I will personally speak with the commandant and ensure that the soldiers tasked are all men who served under Ney. No doubt the royalists will find it amusing, that men so loyal to their former commander should be tasked with his execution."

# Chapter XII: The Pieces are Set

Outside of Orleans, France
5 December 1815

Private, 95th Rifles

The rainy weather that marked the coming of winter in central France felt markedly similar to London to the young rifleman. Born and raised in Southend-on-Sea, he had journeyed to the infamous city, soon after his father's death from tuberculosis, in search of work. It was not long before the recruiting sergeants found him, and he elected to take the 'King's Shilling'. His name was Martin Shepard, and he was a corporal with 1st Battalion of the 95th Rifles. He'd earned his stripes three years after enlisting; partly due to his leadership merits, and partly due to attrition, when his company found itself critically short of non-commissioned officers (NCOs).

Unlike the regular line regiments, the Rifles encouraged both their enlisted men and NCOs to be free-thinkers. Operating in three to four man teams, instead of on a large battle line, riflemen had to be able to react according to rapid situational changes, often in the absence of orders. Both Martin and the riflemen under his charge had been trained to eliminate enemy leaders from a distance with well-placed shots from their Baker rifles, long before the main army engaged. Now, with peace upon Europe for the first time in decades, their task was to watch the roads for robbers and other criminals. It was hardly glorious work, and they had to live in small camps with little more than a tent and a bedroll, while their fellows in the line regiments got to sleep in barracks on actual beds. Still, it was better than being demobilized, like the vast majority of the army, and having to compete for work with a hundred thousand other discharged veterans.

Despite the biting chill of the early morning enshrouded in mist, the campfire outside the corporal's tent kept him surprisingly warm. His haggard green tunic lay across a log next to him, the pair of white corporal's chevrons permanently discoloured with dirt and grass stains brought on by crawling through the tall grass and brush during countless skirmishing engagements. While his uniform was nearly unserviceable, his weapon, though well-worn, was immaculate.

The Baker Rifle was an intricate weapon. Substantially shorter than the standard Land Pattern musket, the rifling cut into the interior of the barrel caused the ball to spin, vastly increasing both range and accuracy. While the average musket had an effective range of perhaps eighty yards with marginal precision, the Baker Rifle was highly accurate at nearly three times the distance. This distinct advantage was tempered by the fact that the rifling fouled up every few rounds and required constant cleaning. It was also very slow to reload. Hence, it was only issued to specialized rifle regiments. Most notable of these were the 60th and 95th Rifles, sometimes called *'the green jackets'* because of the green coats they wore instead of the standard red.

As he ran an oil cloth over the barrel and then function checked the firing mechanism, Martin thought back on the events that had transpired over the past few months. Ever since the fall of Napoleon, all he had had time to do was reminisce. Rather than patrolling the streets of Paris or the other major cities with the rest of the Army of Occupation, the skirmishers of the 95th had been scattered all over the country. Martin and the eight men under his charge were tasked with monitoring a section of road south of Paris, near Orleans, keeping an eye out for bandits and smugglers. Their orders had been so vague, the corporal reckoned unless someone was blatantly causing harm to others, he and his riflemen let them be. Once a week he and two of his men would make their way into the city and report to the lieutenant that was acting as their company commander, their captain having been granted an extended leave in England. Every week Martin would inquire about uniform resupply for his soldiers, and every week the answer was always the same; their command knew of the disrepair of their clothing, and they would rectify the issue as soon as possible. That had been ongoing since August.

"At least I'm able to keep the lads stocked with rations," Martin said to himself, as he leaned his rifle against the log next to his jacket and warmed his hands in the fire. While he dealt with the same discomforts and perpetual boredom as his men, he quietly reckoned, once again, at least it kept him employed. With the wars in Europe and America at an end, tens-of-thousands of recently discharged soldiers would be seeking work. His grandfather had tried to compel him to follow in his profession as a butler, which Martin had scoffed at. Now, as he noted his grimy and cold condition, he figured waiting on toffs was not such a bad way to make a living.

*"Corporal Shepard!"* The voice of his lieutenant snapped him out of his stupor, and Martin was immediately on his feet, reaching for his tunic, which he hurriedly buttoned up. It was unusual for any of the officers to come out and visit the outposts, so he figured it had to be of great importance for his acting commander to have ridden out from Orleans.

"Lieutenant, sir," he said, saluting as the officer walked over to him, while one of the riflemen tended to his horse.

"At ease," his commander said, quickly returning the courtesy. "The major wants to see you. He didn't say why, only that he needs your section for 'special duty'. Damned if I know what it means."

"Yes, sir," Martin replied, "We'll break camp as soon as the lads have had breakfast. Any idea what this duty might entail, sir?"

"He wouldn't say," the lieutenant replied, a trace of annoyance in his voice. "He said something rather vague about the orders coming from Wellington himself."

Army of occupation duty had been rather tedious and boring for Major James Henry Webster of the Grenadier Guards. It had been his regiment at Waterloo, then known as the 1st Regiment of Foot Guards, that had shattered Napoleon's elite Imperial Guard during the closing stages of that brutal encounter. James had fully expected to die that day, even as lines of his decimated companies hammered the French troops with rolling volleys at point-blank range. He was still a captain then, yet with every senior officer either dead or seriously wounded, he had been left in charge of what was left of the battalion. With Wellington himself directing this final action, the British Guards Division, with no small amount of flanking support from the 52nd Oxfordshire, destroyed the Imperial Guard and with them the last hopes of Napoleon's empire.

His fiancé, Emma, had recently returned to Brussels, where the Guards were posted. Yet James had been tasked with garrison duty in Orleans with three companies under his command. One of these, the 1st Company of 3rd Battalion, had been under his command during the year prior to Napoleon's return. He had led them during the first part of the Battle of Quatre Bras, where excessive casualties had led his acting commander to place him in charge of half the battalion.

Given their shared history, he had a special affection for 1st Company, and was continuously frustrated by the lack of replacements, especially in key leadership positions. The former colour sergeant, an Irishman and close friend of Webster's named Patrick Shanahan, had been commissioned a lieutenant at Quatre Bras and had served as acting commander ever since. It was now six months after Waterloo, and they still had no subalterns nor a new colour sergeant. Besides Lieutenant Shanahan, the company had only one sergeant and a pair of corporals to lead their men; half their normal authorizations. And with the lieutenant on leave, First Company had been left under the charge of the ranking NCO, Sergeant James Donaldson. They manned a checkpoint between Orleans and Poitiers, occupying a coaching inn and a few outlying buildings, with the other two companies tasked with patrolling the city itself.

James had left Orleans early in the morning so he could conduct an inspection of the checkpoint. It was two days ride, and he reckoned he would be gone about a week total. The morning, after his arrival, Sergeant Donaldson arranged for an in-ranks inspection of the men. One of the corporals had been left in the company office to go over the payroll for the month, while four privates were on guard duty on either end of the checkpoint. The rest of the company was formed up in four ranks just outside the inn. There should have been roughly a hundred men in the ranks. Yet, even with those wounded at Quatre Bras and Waterloo who had been able to return to duty, there were still less than fifty men standing in the formation. It still saddened the major to know so many of his men had died during those harrowing days, with many more being so badly wounded their injuries forced the army to medically discharge them.

*"Company!"* Sergeant Donaldson shouted, standing in front of the formation. *"Attention!"* He turned to the major and saluted.

It was then that James saw Colonel Stewart riding towards them.

"Look sharp, lads!" a young Irish corporal named David O'Connor shouted, having spotted their battalion commander. It was fortunate the men were already at the position of attention, for it almost looked as if they had been paraded for the colonel's arrival.

"Colonel, sir," James said, saluting as Stewart pulled up the reins on his horse just short of the formation. "A pleasant surprise this."

"Yes, well, I went to your headquarters in Orleans, and your aide told me you were here." Stewart dismounted, returned the major's salute, and then extended his hand. "How are you, James?"

"Well enough, sir." He then said over his shoulder, "Dismiss the company, sergeant."

Sergeant Donaldson saluted and turned to face the men. A few quickly shouted orders and the soldiers went back to their duties.

"I hear you've been made a full colonel," the major noted, as the officers walked towards the door to the inn.

"Only brevetted at the moment," Stewart replied, removing his cane as he tried not to limp in front of the men. "Same with Colonel Askew of $2^{nd}$ Battalion. Let us go inside. We need to talk."

"But of course, sir."

Inside, they tried to give the inn the appearance of normalcy, despite the fact that most of its rooms were occupied by redcoats. James and the colonel went into a side room which the company was using as an office. Behind the desk, going over pay reports was Corporal Christopher Harvey, the only other NCO in the company besides Sergeant Donaldson and Corporal O'Connor. Being one of the few literate soldiers in the company, he had been tasked with many of the administrative functions ever since Sergeant Donaldson assumed temporary command.

"Sirs," he said, quickly rising to his feet. "Apologies for not being out with the lads for inspection. The sergeant said these pay chits were top priority."

"That's fine, corporal," James replied. "Wait outside; the colonel and I need the office."

Harvey saluted sharply and exited the room.

Colonel Stewart took the seat behind the desk, Major Webster sitting across from him. Stewart pulled out an envelope, which he handed to James. Inside was a single sheet.

"Detailed description of a man," James said, as he read. "Approximately six-foot tall, powerful build, ginger hair, wearing a top hat, charcoal grey greatcoat…sir, who is this, and how does he concern us? Is he a robber we need to be on the lookout for?"

"Hardly a robber," Stewart replied. "But yes, you are to be on the lookout for him. Honestly, I have no idea who he is, only that he is of great importance to Wellington."

James perked up at the mention of the Duke's name. He had quite the history with his grace. Their paths crossing numerous times, often under arduous circumstances. Wellington had presented James with his captain's epaulettes after he survived leading the *Forlorn Hope* at the Siege of Badajoz in 1812. During the brief interlude of peace two years later, James had, by chance, managed to save the Duke's life by attacking an assassin who had come at him following a ball. The two rarely spoke. In fact, all Wellington had said after the assassination attempt was for James to fix his trousers that were torn during the scuffle.

"If this person is of such importance to his grace, then is he asking us to provide an escort for him?" he asked, after contemplating the situation.

"No," Stewart replied, shaking his head. "It's all rather secretive, to say the least. Even I don't know most of the details. Suffice it to say, there are certain persons within the French government who want this person dead. Wellington wants him alive and requires us to make sure of it."

"Political cat-and-mouse," James observed. "So this man, whoever he is, will be coming through Poitiers with murderers in pursuit, and Wellington wants us to make certain they do not get him."

"Precisely," the colonel said. "I suspect the pursuers will not be gendarmes, or any persons within the French governmental service. They'll likely find some expendable renegades who no one will miss should their mission go wrong. Have your men keep an eye out for this man over the next few days, and see to it his pursuers are delayed by any means necessary."

Major, Grenadier Guards

With a glass of claret in his hand, the Duke of Wellington reviewed the most recent reports sent in by his division commanders of the Army of Occupation. During the Peninsular War, every report Wellington received could have actionable intelligence that could mean life or death for his army. With peace at last at hand, reports were now mostly tedious and mundane, with nothing unexpected happening from one day to the next. There were two that each had a single line appended to the daily records, which most likely had not even been noticed by their brigade and division commanders. Colonel Stewart of 3/Grenadier Guards and Lieutenant Colonel Barnard of 1/95th Rifles each added the words, *the pieces are set.*

# Chapter XIII: Checkmate

Paris, France
6 December 1815

La Conciergerie, Paris

There had never been any real doubt among the Chamber of Peers as to Marshal Ney's guilt. Most of the testimony had been flippant and irrelevant to the trial at hand. There were a large number of eye-witness accounts of the horrors that had taken place during the Revolution and the atrocities committed therein. While Michel Ney had played no role in any of this, his ties to Napoleon made him guilty by association with the royalists using emotion to sway the peers.

While the heart-wrenching, yet irrelevant, evidence presented by witnesses could have been contested, what damned the marshal most were his own words. Following Napoleon's return to Paris, Ney had penned a message to be distributed to every soldier within the French army, urging them to renounce King Louis and to take up arms in support of Emperor Napoleon once more.

"Marshal Ney is clearly guilty by his own admission!" the Duke of Noailles emphasised. Having lost his wife, daughter, and mother to the guillotine in 1794, he was among many of the royalists who were less than sympathetic towards Ney's plight.

"I agree with the good duke," added the Comte de Polignac, another of the royalist faction. "The commitment of high treason against the king can have only one real punishment…death!"

This lead to a serious of loud ovations and claps of approval from the assembly.

"Marshal Ney is no more guilty of high treason than the lowliest private who refused to shoot the emperor at Lons-le-Saulnier," a noble named Charles Victor, Duc de Broglie, rebuked. Though not a soldier, he was one of the few within the Chambers who still recognized that Ney's actions had always been in the interest of France, rather than one man. "Did he refuse to apprehend Napoleon but instead joined his cause? Absolutely! Yet, so did every soldier sent from Paris to capture or kill the emperor. When Napoleon stood before the soldiers and told them if they wished to kill their emperor, they should do so now, the order was given for the soldiers to fire. Not one did! Instead, they hailed Napoleon as their emperor and as the saviour of France! I am not hear to question whether their actions were right or wrong, but rather to dispute that Marshal Ney abandoned his king through calculated betrayal. His was simply 'desertion in the field', brought on by the love both he and his soldiers had, however misplaced, for the emperor. I, therefore, urge that this body show clemency to a man who both enemy and friend regarded as one of the bravest soldiers to have ever lived."

"Rubbish!" shouted back the Comte de Polignac. "Michel Ney was a general and a Marshal of France, not to mention made a duke by Napoleon. Does a man of such eminence and rank take his orders from unruly enlisted men? Would he have ever ceased to order his men into battle, simply because the privates were scared and did not wish to go? No, I say!"

As Ney watched the proceedings draw to their preconceived conclusion, he knew he had committed a grievous error by having his trial moved from military tribunal to the Chamber of Peers. Aside from the Duc de Broglie's latest remarks, any defence of the marshal had been tepid at best, whereas the calls for his guilt and damnation were overwhelming. That he was guilty, there could be no doubt. However, it was now up to the Chambers to decide whether he lived or died. With so many of the peers overly wrought with emotion, it was doubtful that any would bother to heed, or even acknowledge, the recently-signed Treaty of Paris and its forbidding of capital sentences to the emperor's former marshals.

There was much haste to finish the trial and be done with it, and so the members of the Chambers stayed well into the night with the votes being cast around midnight. Ney was brought before the Chambers floor, where the Duke of Richelieu read the results.

"In the trial of Michel Ney, Marshal of France, on the charge of high treason, the verdict of the Chamber of Peers is as follows," Richelieu began, *"152 votes, guilty with a sentence of death; 17 votes, guilty with a sentence of exile; 5 votes abstained, and 1 vote of not guilty.* Therefore, the Chamber of Peers finds Marshal Ney guilty of high treason and sentences him to be executed by firing squad tomorrow at 9 o'clock."

Ney said nothing and was quickly ushered from the hall. Most of the peers looked overjoyed, particularly the royalists who had lost family members during the Revolution and somehow felt vindicated. Those marshals who were amongst the peers looked utterly dejected. Whether they had voted for death, exile, or abstained, Ney would never know. He could only assume that, given his staunch defence of him at the very end, Charles Victor, Duc de Broglie was the one man to vote for his acquittal.

As soon as Ney was ushered out of the chamber, it was de Broglie who addressed the assembly one last time. In a voice full of venom and spite he said, "Had you, who sat in judgment upon Marshal Ney, been a body of peasants who had braved fire and sword for the Bourbon cause, this sentence of death might have been pronounced with pure, though stern, lips," he exclaimed. "Instead, it remains a deep disgrace to France that among the peers who voted not only for Ney's condemnation but for his death, are some who had yourselves accepted office and pay from Napoleon during the Hundred Days. A pox on this unworthy house!"

With sentence passed and escape now impossible, Michel Ney, Marshal of France, wanted nothing more than to spend his last few hours on earth with his wife and sons. Aglae brought the boys to see him in his cell, and though she did her best to maintain a brave face in front of the children, Michel could clearly see she was breaking inside. She knew Wellington's meeting with King Louis had not gone well, and word had quickly spread about the sentence of the Chambers. Though it be a profound diplomatic blight for the Bourbons and for France, it was too late for it to matter to Ney and his family. All that remained was to wait until morning, when the marshal would be taken to the execution square to be shot like a common criminal.

Their oldest sons, Joseph and Michel, were twelve and eleven, respectively. Eugene was seven, with the youngest, Edgar, barely three. Ney embraced the lads closely, cherishing these last few minutes suddenly regretting he had not been there for more of their young lives. Though immensely proud of who their father was, they scarcely knew him. This did not stop the oldest from attempting to defend the family's honour.

"I hear you challenged the Duke of Wellington to a duel," Ney said to Joseph.

"Yes, sir," the lad said, his head held high. "He brought about the fall of France, as well as that of my father."

"No," Michel replied, gently shaking his head. "Wellington was simply a soldier who did his duty, like your father. At least with him there was honesty, for I always knew he was my enemy. Do not hate a man who is forthright enough to publicly give you his enmity. Instead, beware of those treacherous enough to publicly claim to be your friend while conspiring like Judas behind you."

The boy nodded in understanding then embraced his father. He had held up bravely for his mother and his younger brothers, but now the tears fell, and he found he could not speak.

"It's alright, my son," Michel said soothingly. "Not all tears are in vain."

He reached up for his wife, who sat beside him and their sons. She rested her head on his shoulder as he placed his arm around her. Aglae sobbed quietly, while keeping her handkerchief up by her eyes. Michel rocked her gently as his sons held onto him desperately, as if he were the last refuge from a sinking ship. In those moments, the family did their best to make peace with their fate, and as Ney kissed his wife for the last time he whispered to her, "Until we meet again, my dearest love."

It was after 2 o'clock when Aglae and her sons left Michel's cell. The marshal then longed for nothing but sleep, so that the morning would come more quickly. He hoped for dreams of his beloved wife, in a happier time, away from the sorrows of war and death.

"Excuse me, marshal," one of the guards said, rousing him from his slumber.

Ney looked up and saw the man's face was full of vexation. He was a former member of the Imperial Guard, the very regiments who had assaulted the heights at the climax of the Battle of Waterloo, only to be shot to pieces by the British Guards Division that lay waiting for them in the tall grass.

"What is it?" the marshal asked impatiently. He wished for sleep, not because he was fatigued, but rather to expedite his eventual fate. If he was to die, then he wished to simply get it over with. Still, he found he pitied the soldier, who had gone through the same torments on the battlefield as he, only to now have to take part in the execution of his former commander.

"There's someone here to see you, sir."

Ney glowered at the man who walked into the cell and removed his hat. "I had hoped that my last visions on this earth would be of my wife and children," he snarled. "A pity that it should be you instead."

"If you think I have come here to gloat over a fallen enemy, then you know me not," Wellington retorted.

"Then why are you here? Is it about my son challenging you to a duel?"

"Don't be ridiculous!" Wellington snapped. "The boy was only trying to save his family's honour. You and I both know he'd be better suited challenging the king."

"At least that fat bastard would be too slow for him with a pistol or sword," Michel said with a chuckle of macabre humour, as he leaned back in the corner of the room and folded his arms across his chest. "Why are you here then?"

"Your conviction and sentence are a travesty of justice," the Duke replied. He remained standing, his eyes fixed on his former adversary.

"Yes, I suppose I should thank you for heeding my wife's pleas that you attempt to compel the king to commute my sentence," Ney replied, his tone softening. In truth, he did not hate Wellington. He privately acknowledged that his feelings of envy toward the Duke, for defeating both he and Napoleon, were unbecoming of a true gentleman.

"A pity, then, that your words fell upon deaf ears," Ney continued.

"Even a king is not above the law," Wellington insisted. "The Treaty of Paris *is* the law, signed by the king's own ministers. And if Louis and the Chamber of Peers refuse to abide by it, then they must be made to do so."

"How?" Ney was genuinely confused as he sat upright. Surely Wellington would not use British soldiers to halt the execution by force!

"Three men will be coming soon to take you to the place of execution," Wellington explained. "They are officers under my command. One of them, Sir Robert Wilson, you've met before. In fact, you fought against him at the Battle of Puerto de Baños."

Ney smirked at the irony. "And what is his significance to me in this affair?"

"All will be explained soon enough," the Duke replied. "But know this, Michel, *death is just the beginning.*"

Wellington's cryptic words sat uneasily with the marshal. In reality, he had said nothing other than Ney's sentence violated law, and that three of the Duke's own men would come to take him to the execution square. He was rather surprised, though, that Wellington had called him by his given name. Michel decided there was nothing more to be accomplished by dwelling on the matter, and allowed himself to fall into a deep sleep once more.

At the barracks, General Sir Robert Wilson, along with his fellow officers, Bruce and Hutchinson, met with the commandant. Though the execution was not set to take place until well into the morning, it seemed that no one involved would be sleeping this night.

"You're men are ready to do their duty?" Sir Robert asked the commandant.

"They are," the officer replied, "though it is a rather hateful task for all of them. The king found it a good jest that it be Ney's own soldiers who execute him. But, yes, they are all good soldiers and will do what must be done."

"I understand there was a change in the time of execution," Wilson remarked.

"That is true," the commandant, who was one of Ida Sainte-Elme's contacts, confirmed. "The minister of police agrees that we should expedite Marshal Ney's passing, lest the public sight of him being shot should provoke unrest."

"A sound plan," Wilson agreed.

"We'd like to meet with the firing squad," Hutchinson said, "as well as the officer who will be commanding them."

"Of course," the commandant replied. "I have a young lieutenant who, in fact, fought his first actions at Quatre Bras and Waterloo, who will be commanding the mission. He is aided by a steady sergeant who won't falter."

"We'd like to meet with him," Wilson said.

"Of course."

The three British officers were led outside, then down a flight of steps into a basement. Inside, the lieutenant, sergeant, and seven privates were taking their time getting into their uniforms. It would be a sombre day for them. All were veterans who served under Marshal Ney at various times; two of them, like the gaoler at the Conciergerie, were former members of the Imperial Guard who fought beside the marshal at Waterloo.

"Where are their weapons?" Sir Robert asked.

"Down the hall, room on the left," the commandant answered. He excused himself, saying he had both the mayor of Paris, as well as several members of the king's cabinet, meeting him later in the morning and he needed to get some sleep.

General Wilson addressed the young lieutenant. "When your men are ready, we will go with you to the Conciergerie. You may wish to address them now."

The lieutenant nodded and turned to his men. "Vous les hommes tout servi sous le Maréchal Ney," he said. "Vous l'avez tous aimé. Mais maintenant que vous devez faire votre devoir, pour la France."

"What did he just say to them?" Bruce whispered to Wilson.

"He said, 'you all served with Marshal Ney'," the general replied quietly. "You all loved him. But now you must do your duty, for France."

"Pour la France!" the sergeant of the firing squad emphasized. His voice was breaking, and Wilson thought he could see a tear forming in his eye.

The British general motioned for the man to come over to him. "You and your men may not feel any recoil from your muskets," Sir Robert explained, "but rest assured that Marshal Ney will lie dead."

The French NCOs mouth twitched slightly, comprehending what the British officer was saying. "My men will not ask any questions, sir."

While Sir Robert continued speaking with the men of the firing squad, Bruce and Hutchinson walked down the hall and found the table with eight muskets laid across, along with the cartridges to be used for the execution.

"Let's get these things loaded," Bruce said, grabbing the first musket and cartridge. They followed normal loading procedure, priming the flash pan with a small amount of powder, then pouring the rest down the barrel. But instead of dropping the ball in, they wadded up the paper cartridge and jammed it down the barrel, where it would act as wadding to keep the powder in place.

"We'd better do something about these," Hutchinson said with a chuckle, tossing one of the musket balls up in the air and catching it once more.

"And we should probably sort the officer's pistol out," Bruce added. "Just in case." He pulled out his knife and pried away on the flint that was held in place by a small claw in the hammer. It soon popped loose, and Bruce placed it in his small satchel along with all of the musket balls. They returned to the meeting room where the soldiers were donning their shakos and tightening their cross belts. Bruce gave a subtle nod to General Wilson.

"Récupérez vos armes," the lieutenant said to his men.

The sergeant led them down the hall, and soon each returned with a musket over his shoulder. The NCO handed the pistol to his officer. Soon they would be departing for the Conciergerie.

"The muskets are all properly loaded, sir," Bruce said, as the three British officers stepped out into the cold night air.

"And what of the officer's pistol?" Sir Robert asked.

"Loading it with a blank would be dangerous," Hutchinson answered. "Placed up against the skull, the force of a fired blank could still be fatal. So I popped the flint out instead. I doubt he'll want to wait around for half an hour while someone runs back to barracks and gets him another one."

"I hope you're right," Wilson replied. "Still, I will try and coax things along quickly so it doesn't even come to that. Right, well let us go and meet the good marshal then!"

# Chapter XIV: The Execution

Paris, France
7 December 1815

The Execution of Marshal Ney

It was still dark out when the cell door opened, awakening the marshal. The execution was set to take place at 9 o'clock, and it was clearly far too early for the escorts to have come for him.

"Marshal Ney," a man said, removing his hat. He wore a heavy cloak, though underneath Ney could just make out the scarlet tunic he wore. "I am Sir Robert Wilson, an honour to meet you at last."

He extended his hand which the marshal accepted. He then turned back to his two companions, one of whom carried a large gunnysack.

"What time is it?" the marshal asked.

"Five in the morning," Sir Robert replied. "The king has been compelled to move up the time of execution. He fears you still possess the love of the people and shooting you in public would unsettle the populace."

"I see," Ney replied with a nod. "Then I should don my marshal's uniform and make the best of the end."

"No, I'm afraid your uniform would be too conspicuous," the British general replied, shaking his head. He nodded to his fellow soldiers. The one with the sack pulled out a bladder full of dark fluid. "You will place this under your shirt, but be careful you don't rupture it too soon."

Ney was handed the bladder, which he turned over in his hands. It was very thin and leaking slightly around the tied end.

"When the time comes, ask that you be allowed to give the order," Sir Robert continued. "When you tell the firing squad to aim for your heart, smash the bladder with your fist and fall as soon as they fire. We've made certain their weapons are all loaded with blanks."

"Every last one of them are former soldiers from your command, including the Imperial Guard," Hutchinson explained. "Trust me, they'll not be asking any questions."

"But surely the doctor will see I am not dead," Ney observed. "And there is always an officer on hand to finish off the condemned with a pistol shot to the head. One cannot exactly fake a man's brains blowing out the side of his head with a bladder full of pig's blood."

"Yes...well, let's just say not everyone involved with the execution may have been informed of the time change," Wilson replied. "And flintlock pistols are notorious for misfiring." He then drew a knife. "What we do need to do is cut some holes in your shirt. Sorry to ruin it, but it must look like you've been shot."

Ney's heart raced as he was escorted out of the jail cell to the waiting carriage. The soldiers of the firing squad stood on either side and, with a command from their lieutenant, they all snapped to attention and saluted the marshal with their muskets. He made sure he returned the salute, touching his hand to the brim of his top hat. He also kept his greatcoat closed about him, lest anyone should see the holes in his shirt, or the sticky pig's blood that was already started to ooze out of the bladder.

Michel was partly filled with doubt, his mind conjuring that this was all a wicked ruse to toy with his emotions just before his death. And yet, he knew deep down inside that Wellington was not a man to make such a cruel jest. The marshal looked around into the gloomy fog of the Paris night. Oil lamps cast an eerie glow, reflecting off the shako plates of the soldiers who surrounded him. Their faces were wrought with emotion. Some even had tears rolling down their cheeks. Clearly they did not relish the hateful task they were being ordered to perform. The sorrowful display also told Ney these men were likely not aware of Wellington's ploy.

A priest accompanied them, holding a Bible open to the Psalms, which he recited quietly while walking beside the condemned.

When they reached the carriage, Ney turned to the priest. "Get in, father," he said. "Afterwards, I will go first."

The priest complied and climbed in, still reciting his prayers. Ney sat across from him with his hands folded in his lap. His top hat sat cocked slightly atop his head, knocked aside by the marshal's great height as he entered the carriage. It felt strange to him to be dressed as such, instead of in his marshal's uniform. If he was to die, then he wanted to be garbed as a soldier.

It was a ten minute ride to the execution square at Grenelle Barrier, yet the carriage stopped after a short ride of just three hundred yards, near the Luxembourg Garden.

"Why are we stopped?" Ney asked.

No one replied. Instead, the door was jerked open from the outside, and an officer signalled for him to get out.

The execution of Marshal Ney was to be a rather public affair, yet here they were, in a small enclosure that was still under construction, where only a few witnesses stood waiting. Strangely enough, almost all of these people were British, including a member of the English Parliament named Quintin Dick. He had been informed of the time change of execution by the Duke of Wellington, who asked him to go and act as a witness on behalf of His Majesty's government. Dick, who had never been a soldier, was morbidly fascinated to observe the death of a man so famous for his personal bravery.

"Bandez les yeux??" a soldier said, asking Ney if he wished for a blindfold while holding up the piece of black cloth.

The marshal simply shook his head. Another came forward with a section of rope to bind his hands, though he stopped short, as he was suddenly made nervous by Ney's hard stare.

"At least allow me to die with honour," he said calmly, "and not like some common horse thief."

The soldier looked over to his officer, who gave an affirmative nod.

"I ask one last thing," Ney said to the officer. "These men were once my soldiers; allow me to give the order to fire."

"Of course," the young lieutenant said. The man was clearly distraught, and at least partially relieved he would not have to give the order to kill a man he deeply regarded as a hero.

Ney walked slowly towards the wall, removing his hat, which he tossed onto the ground, and staring at the cold, lifeless rock that almost seemed to beckon him. Wellington's words felt distant, almost as if they had been little more than a dream. He placed his hand over his heart and felt the bladder that was slowly leaking against his skin. He inhaled deeply through his nose, breathing in the dampness of the early predawn of a cold December day. He then turned and gazed at the small crowd of onlookers, most of whom were gathered by the gate to the gardens across the narrow street. He made eye contact with the soldiers who stood in two ranks before him.

"Soldiers," he said in a strong voice that echoed off the wall behind him. "When I give the command, fire straight at my heart. Wait for the order, for it will be my last to you. I protest against my condemnation. I have fought a hundred battles for France, and not one against her." He then nodded to the officer, who drew his sword.

*"Premier rang, s'agenouiller!"* the lieutenant said, the soldiers in the front rank kneeling. *"Préparez-vous ... présente!"* He looked towards Ney for one last moment before turning his head away.

Eight muskets were now pointed at Marshal Ney, who raised his left hand high. He took what appeared to be his last breath and smashed his fist against his chest.

"Soldiers...*fire!*"

The volley of musket fire was almost deafening to the witnesses, who jumped at the loud crack that now rang in their ears. The smoke slowly cleared and Marshal Ney lay face first on the ground, his arms down by his sides, blood pooling around the edges of his body.

"Well, that was strange," Dick said to Sir Robert Wilson, who appeared to be the only spectator not startled by the burst of gunfire.

"What do you mean?" the general asked.

"It's just that…eight musket shots at close range should have sent him sprawling backwards. In the least, I expected the body would twitch or convulse, something like that. He just fell flat on his face." The MP was clearly confused, not seeing what he had expected.

"Not every man who is shot makes a theatrical show of it," Wilson replied. He then asked, "Do you have your vial?"

"Oh, yes!" Dick said excitedly, pulling a small glass tube with a cork stopper out of his coat. Many of the British witnesses brought vials or rags with which to sop up some of the marshal's blood. It may have appeared macabre to some that they would view the blood of an executed man as a type of memento. Yet, it also showed the level of awe and respect they held for *'the bravest of the brave'*.

Wilson was the only one not to take part. Instead, he quickly walked over to the guards' commander, who had yet to draw his pistol to give the body the compulsory *coup de grace* shot to the head. The civilian spectators, being mostly British, were unaware of this requirement, nor did they notice the lack of the doctor who was supposed to officially declare the marshal deceased.

"Retirez le corps," Wilson said to the officer. "Laisser le Maréchal de France de conserver sa dignité." His orders, to remove the body and allow the Marshal of France to maintain his dignity, were hastily followed by the soldiers, without even waiting for confirmation from their officer. Ney's body was picked up by his limbs and Wilson noted how he remained perfectly limp. He quietly hoped no one had bothered to check the weapons of the firing squad to ensure they were loaded properly. A terrible end it would be if anyone had reloaded the muskets!

He was reassured when he heard Quintin Dick reiterate once more, "He didn't even twitch. Not so much as a sigh."

# Chapter XV: Where Liberty Has Arisen

Davidson, North Carolina
July, 1840

Seal of Davidson College

It was a busy time for Peter, who refused to let the effects of his advancing years slow him. Now seventy-one years of age, he was not able to fence like he once did, and he now required assistance when mounting his horse. His body constantly ached; old injuries from another life finally taking their toll. Yet for all that, he found himself traveling more now and taking a far more active role in the education community. He had thought to, perhaps, go into retirement. Instead, he was being given the honour of presenting diplomas to the first graduating class from Davidson College, founded three years prior.

Named for Brigadier General William Lee Davidson of the American Revolution, who was killed at the Battle of Cowan's Ford in 1781, the board of trustees had approached Peter Ney and asked him to design the seal for them. As an old soldier with a reputation for nobility and purpose, he was ideally suited to create something that would embody the spirit of the new college.

Peter had spent several months going through a number of differing designs. Finally he decided on a fist holding a dagger which, in turn, was wrapped by a serpent. A glowing star was placed above the fist, with the encompassing circle around the seal bearing the Latin phrase, *'Alenda Lux Ubi Orta Libertas'*, meaning *'Let Learning Be Cherished Where Liberty Has Arisen'*.

"Strong, yet noble," a trustee told him, when Peter presented his sketches to the board.

The old school teacher had a more personal reason for attending the ceremony on that hot July day. Among the eleven seniors receiving their diplomas was young Alexander Reille. Though receiving his degree in mathematics, he had also taken his former headmaster's advice and studied foreign languages in depth. He kept in touch with Peter over the years since he left Mocksville and, in his own way, the old teacher viewed him as a friend. Whether it was his attachment to the name of Reille or that Alexander had simply been that good of a student, he could not say. What he did know, was that a young man who had once studied under him was among the first class of graduates at the college whose seal he had the privilege of designing.

There were, perhaps, a hundred guests on hand to witness the first group of graduates from the college. Among them was the Governor of North Carolina, with most of the rest being either friends or family of the seniors.

"Family, friends, distinguished guests," the dean said, as he took to the speaker's podium. "We have the privilege today of having the man who designed our very seal present these diplomas. He served as a soldier under Napoleon Bonaparte, and for more than twenty years he has served the education community as both teacher and headmaster to many of our best and brightest students. Ladies and gentlemen, I give you Peter Stuart Ney."

The crowd clapped graciously for the old schoolteacher and soldier, who waved to them before taking his place beside the dean. A member of the faculty would then hand the diplomas to Peter, who would, in turn, present them to the graduates as their names were called. He was beaming with pride when Alexander Reille's name was called.

"You have made me very proud," Peter said quietly, as he clasped Reille's hand while handing his rolled diploma to him. "It is an honour to present this to you."

"L'honneur est pour moi," Alexander replied in French, stating that the honour was his. He leaned in and said quietly, "Il a été un privilège, Maréchal de France."

Peter simply nodded and smiled. That the young man had addressed him in French as 'Marshal of France' was likely in reference to the jest they used to share, when in Alexander's early days he had noted that both he and his schoolmaster shared the surnames of famous Napoleonic generals. And yet, there was a knowing look in the young man's eye that told Peter there was something far more significant to the remark.

Peter arrived back in Mocksville late in the afternoon, three days following the graduation ceremony at Davidson College. As he rode slowly past the house of an old friend, Mister Stephen Austin, a noted carpenter, he tipped his hat to Madam Susan Austin.

"Good day to you, madam," he said.

"And to you, Mister Ney," she said with a curtsey. "Would you do us the honour of paying a visit to my husband and me? You must be tired and thirsty after your long ride."

"Delighted," Peter replied.

Susan first thought to help the old man from his horse, but he managed well enough, albeit a bit slowly.

"And how was the ceremony at the college?" she asked. The Austins' oldest son was soon coming of age and had high aspirations to attend the new centre of learning.

"Splendid," Peter replied as Madam Austin led him into the house. "And my former students are well, I take it?"

"Splendid," Susan mimicked with a smile. While her husband had been one of Peter's students many years before, she had also attended many of his lectures as a young woman. She brought him a glass of water with lemon and left him for a moment while he sat in their front drawing room. Returning a minute later she said, "Stephen is just finishing up a project and said he will be in shortly."

Peter nodded in reply, and while waiting for his former pupil, he and Susan talked at length about the days when she and her then-future husband studied under the mysterious soldier from France.

"Do you wish you could return home, even now?" Susan asked.

Peter nodded slowly. "Every day," he replied. "I don't mind talking about it anymore, though to be honest, I have never stopped mourning the loss of my wife and sons…they're not dead, mind you. It's just that I have not seen them in twenty-five years."

"What's to stop you from returning now?" Susan asked. "You told us you were a soldier of Napoleon. Well, your old enemies, the Bourbons are long gone. The House of Orleans under Louis-Philippe has ruled France for ten years now."

"The Bourbons may no longer rule France, but they have seen to it that I can never return," Peter explained. It was clear he still did not wish to divulge too much about his past to her, yet he still had things he needed to discuss. "As long as I live in America, any danger that may still exist falls upon me alone. If I were to show up in France again, my wife and sons would be threatened as well. Believe me, my dear, old enmities run deep and are tempered by neither time nor a change in monarch. A time will come, when someone will have to return to France in my stead, but not yet. It will come when my hour has grown late."

The door that lead from the back kitchen to the attached shop opened with a loud creak and Stephen entered, wiping his hands on an old rag.

"I thought I heard voices in here," he said boisterously, as his former teacher slowly rose from his seat. Stephen extended his hand. "Mister Ney, a pleasure to see you, as always!"

"Please, the pleasure is all mine," Peter replied, accepting Stephen's hand. "Your darling wife tells me you are finishing a new project."

"Oh, yes," Mister Austin replied. "I was just wiping some of the spilled oil off my hands. Would you like to come have a look? It might be a bit macabre, but you will appreciate the craftsmanship."

Stephen took Peter into his workshop. Despite the large number of saws, awls, chisels, and other wood-working implements, as well as various stacked cords of lumber, the shop was surprisingly immaculate. Stephen had said that he picked up his old schoolmaster's obsession for order, and so his shop could never be in disarray. In the centre of the shop, balanced on three sawhorses was a rather large oak coffin.

"Just finished staining it," Stephen explained. "I've got some decorative accents that I still need to finish."

"Exquisite craftsmanship," Peter said approvingly. "It's rather large, too, I see."

"Yes, well the fellow who commissioned the job is a rather big man. I'd say he's about your height and build."

"The coffin would be a good fit for you," Susan said with a soft laugh.

"Ah," Peter replied, laughing at the quip. "They once thought of putting me in a coffin, but they were wrong!"

## Chapter XVI: Death is Just the Beginning

Paris, France
7 December 1815
\*\*\*

Ney's body ached from the impact of the fall, his cheek was bruised, and his arms and legs felt like they had been wrenched out of their sockets. His teeth had cut the inside of his cheek when he landed on the cobblestones, with the drool of blood coming from his mouth adding to the authenticity of the ordeal. He remained completely limp as he was carried by several soldiers to the waiting cart.

*Death is just the beginning*, he thought to himself as he lay in the back of the wagon. A canvas tarp had been thrown over him. It was thick, and stunk of the pig carcasses it had previously covered, and made him itch. Still, his discomfort was a small price to pay for having denied King Louis the pleasure of his death. No doubt word was already spreading that Marshal Ney's execution had been moved up several hours, and had taken place near the Luxembourg Gardens. Ney remained perfectly still, lest some nosy passers-by managed to lift the tarp and gaze upon his mortal remains.

The wagon rolled along the cobblestones, jarring the marshal with every rut and gouge the hard wheels bounced over. It was approximately three miles from the Luxembourg Gardens to the hospice; a short journey that would have taken at least an hour during the daytime congestion. Ney was reminded of this mentally, and he was grateful the conspirators had had the time of execution changed. The sound and feel of the rolling wagon levelling out, along with a chance hint of damp air told him they were crossing the River Seine. Ten minutes later, the wagon came to a halt; the horses' whinnying adding an almost dramatic feel.

Ney remained perfectly still, scarcely even allowing himself to breathe as the tarp was thrown off and he was dragged, rather unceremoniously, from the back. Given his rather immense size, it took four sets of hands to carry him, one on each limb. He heard a number of voices talking quietly. Though he dared not open his eyes even a little, he knew there were at least a handful of onlookers who caught word of the early execution and had come to see the body of the slain marshal. More would come throughout the day as word reached the city's populace. He smiled inside, knowing the sight of his limp body, covered in blood, would add to the deception. He also wasn't sure how many, if any, of those who now dealt with the disposal of his body were even aware of the fraud; that the man they carried was not dead at all. As such, he let his body remain completely immobile, despite the cramping of his arms, legs, and back as he was carried like a carcass through the slaughterhouse.

He heard the doors to the hospice open with a loud creak as he was carried inside, the men carrying him panting as they struggled with his dead weight. His body was dumped onto a heavy oak table, where countless other corpses had been laid out while awaiting burial. The large doors leading outside were shut, and Ney thought he heard a key locking them.

"You're safe now, marshal," a woman's voice said gently.

For the first time since he'd ordered the soldiers to fire, Michel opened his eyes. The woman, who he could only assume was Sister Therese, smiled at him warmly. He guessed her age as somewhere in her late forties, and she wore a simple head scarf rather than the impractical nun's habit. She had on a heavy grey apron over her plain dress, and as he dared himself to sit up, she removed her gloves.

"Risen from the dead," Ney said, with a trace of macabre humour.

The sister did not laugh.

"Your friends have left you a change of shirt," she replied, "though there is little to be done about your trousers and great coat. Here is a scarf, keep it wrapped around your head, at least until you are out of Paris."

The marshal stood and tried to stretch out his aching limbs. He saw the large coffin on the far side of the large room. He walked over and saw a large canvas sack stuffed with what he guessed was rocks, potatoes, and other things to give it density and weight.

"Wouldn't due for the grave party to have a coffin that was an empty box," Therese explained. "You're a rather big man, marshal, though not in the corpulent sense like that disgrace who now sits upon the throne of France."

"I should wait until after this is taken away before I depart," he observed, nodding towards the coffin. "I suspect our audience waiting outside these doors will only grow larger throughout the day."

"You can be rest assured of that," the sister replied. "But they will disperse soon enough, once they think you're being moved to the cemetery, with many of them following the coffin to its grave. Only the gravedigger knows of the scheme."

At Ney's raised eyebrow of concern she was quick to explain.

"No one would believe that a frail woman of my size hefted a six-foot beast like yourself into his casket, not when it took four men to drag you in here. Not to worry, the gravedigger is a friend, and none of the others at this hospice are aware of the situation."

"I am indebted to you, sister," Ney said, as he took the change of shirt from her.

"It is God who preserved you," she replied. "Give thanks unto the Lord, marshal. Clearly He has some other purpose for you in this life."

One Frenchman who witnessed the execution was Fouche's deputy, Javier Foss. He had stood away from the others, keeping a watchful eye from over by the carriage, behind the firing squad. As the marshal fell, he immediately suspected what most of the English witnesses had not. Foss had seen his share of executions, and even taken part in a few. Like Quintin Dick had said, he knew that close-range fire from numerous large calibre muskets would have sent Ney sprawling backwards. Another subtle detail that Foss picked up on was the lack of recoil on the muskets themselves. The force generated by firing such a weapon was jarring, yet not one of the soldiers so much as flinched. And then there was the matter of the British officer immediately spiriting the body away before the commander could perform the necessary *coup de grace*. Whether the young lieutenant was simply overwhelmed, or worse, complicit in the farce, Foss' superiors would need to know immediately.

"Have that officer arrested as soon as he's returned to barracks," Foss said to one of his men who'd accompanied him. The deputy police minister had to make his report at once.

He found Fouche at the palace, where the king was just finishing his breakfast; a gorging feast that would have fed three normal people. Also present was Prime Minister Richelieu and the Prince de Talleyrand.

"The traitor's dead, is he?" King Louis asked, as he stuffed a pickled egg into his bulbous mouth. "I would like to have witnessed his end personally, though my ministers feel my presence would have been in poor taste."

"Ney is not dead, sire," Foss said, grimacing.

The king almost choked as he coughed up pieces of egg. Fouche's face turned red with anger.

"What do you mean, *not dead*? Explain yourself, man!"

"Treachery, sir," Foss replied. "None of those blind Englishmen seemed to notice, but I did. The soldiers' weapons were loaded with blanks, the commander did not finish the traitor with the required shot to the head, and no doctor was present. I've ordered the commanding officer to be arrested."

Louis' face was purple, almost as if he were choking, though it was an expression of utter rage.

"This is Wellington's doing," he snarled. "That damned Englishman is making a mockery of me!" He slammed his fist down on the table, his anger boiling over. He then turned to his prime minister. "Richelieu, have the Duke brought to me immediately!"

"Yes, sire." The prime minister bowed and quickly stepped from the room.

The king turned his glare on Fouche. "Finish this, Fouche," he said slowly, his voice dripping with utter malice. "As far as the public is concerned, Ney the traitor lies dead. You *will* see to it that he stays in his grave!"

It took Richelieu the better part of two hours to locate Wellington. The Duke was eventually found out on the parade grounds, performing a mounted inspection of the 1st Dragoon Guards. Each trooper was dressed smartly in red tunic with gold and black accents, with white baldrics strapped across their chests. Each had donned grey trousers, as well as their plumed black and gold helmets. All carried both carbine, as well as sabre, which they had drawn and resting on their right shoulders.

"Wellington!" Richelieu shouted as he rode out onto the field. "I must speak with you at once!"

Wellington continued to ride down the line, acting almost as if he had not heard the man. When he reached the end of the line, he turned his horse about and addressed the French prime minister.

"Like you, I am a duke, and will be addressed as such."

"Forgive me, your grace," Richelieu replied. "Please, I must speak with you at once. It is urgent."

"I am in the middle of inspecting His Britannic Majesty's dragoons," Wellington replied calmly. "Ensuring their readiness in maintaining the safety of both your realm and ours is what is urgent." Though he gave nothing away by either his words or expression, the duke knew exactly why the prime minister had come to see him. Had the king not so grievously insulted him, he may have paused in his inspection and given Richelieu his attention.

An hour passed, and the prime minister watched impatiently as Wellington and the Dragoons' commander rode down the lines of troopers. He wondered if the duke was purposely taking his time, asking frequent questions of both the colonel and his men, in order to purposely delay him. At last, he rode to the front of the formation and gave the colonel leave to dismiss his men. The two exchanged salutes, and Wellington then turned about and rode over to Richelieu.

"Now, my dear duke," he said, in a calm voice that contrasted the prime minister's frantic expression. "What can I do for you?"

"The king summons you. You are to attend him at once."

"Am I now?" Wellington's face remained unchanged.

Richelieu knew, after Louis' horrid insult, it would be difficult compelling Wellington to do anything the king requested. Though required to be diplomatic and accommodating, the Duke did not answer to the French king.

"Please, your grace," the prime minister pleaded. "It's about the execution of Marshal Ney."

"And what does his majesty need to see me about that?" Wellington asked. "The good marshal lies dead and has likely already been taken away for burial. His execution, I should remind you, was in direct violation of the Treaty of Paris. A flouting of international convention is scarcely a good way for France to re-join the world stage, and the king should think himself lucky that King George will likely overlook the matter. Provided, of course, it is left alone and not brought to the attention of his representatives."

"Will you, at least, convey your assessments to his majesty?" Richelieu was becoming rather desperate.

King Louis was no doubt becoming very impatient waiting for him, and if he failed to bring the Duke it would make for a hellish audience.

"You're the king's prime minister," Wellington replied. "I have conveyed my assessments to you, his chief representative. Were he to continue in his insistence of a personal meeting, I would feel compelled to greet him with the same level of courtesy he showed the Duke of Wellington just yesterday."

Richelieu found it strange that Wellington would sometimes refer to himself in the third person, though, in this case, it did emphasize the caustic diplomatic blunder the king had made. All of Europe, most of all the king, knew he owed his restoration to the Duke. Wellington was not a man to overtly remind the king of this. However, this latest exchange with Louis' prime minister made it clear the Duke of Wellington did not answer to King Louis XVIII of France, and at no time would he accept direct orders from the king. It also spelled out there would be consequences, however subtle, for insulting the very man who'd saved his kingdom from the usurper, Bonaparte.

Prime Minister Richelieu could not say if Wellington's firm rebuke made him complicit in the faked execution of Marshal Ney. What he did know, was the duke would never again demean himself by being in the presence of King Louis.

As he turned his horse to leave the parade field and return to the palace, Wellington called out to him once more.

"I hear the commander of the guard was arrested. I suggest you release him at once, for there is nothing with which he can be charged. Michel Ney, Marshal of France, lies dead. It would be best if he were left in peace."

# Chapter XVII: The Empty Casket

Paris, France
7 December 1815
***

Despite the veiled warnings from Wellington, there was no peace to be had in the royal court regarding Marshal Ney. The king was in a panic, though his ministers did their best to keep the matter quiet. If word were to get out that Ney lived and the execution a farce, it would be a catastrophic embarrassment to the king. The lieutenant who conducted the execution would be soon released, for as Richelieu had told the king, if he was innocent of any wrongdoing, it would be ill-advised for him to know of the treachery. He would, instead, be given a formal reprimand for failing to follow all procedures during an execution and then returned to his duties. The immediate crisis, however, was what to do about the escaped marshal himself.

"If Ney has acquired a horse, he could be miles from Paris by now," Fouche lamented as he and Foss walked towards the gaol.

"Not to fear," his deputy consoled him. "I'll have a handful of our fastest mounts ready for our 'associates'. I suspect he will head for the coast, either Rochefort or Bordeaux."

The entered the gaol and, along with the warden, walked down the stone steps into the depths below. It was cold, and dank, and always smelled of mould. At the bottom of the steps was an open room with several passages that led to the actual gaol cells. A dozen filthy men were gathered here, armed guards surrounding them. All were hardened criminals; rapists, thieves, murderers, all. As such, they were deemed expendable and also ideal for this mission.

"Gentlemen," Fouche said, practically sneering as he said the word. "All of you have been found guilty of the most heinous of crimes against the people of France. As such, the hangman's noose awaits every last one of you. However, we are offering a chance for each of you to attain the king's pardon."

"Piss on the king," one of the men spat.

This was immediately met with a hard blow across the back of the head from a guard's musket.

"Take that man away and have him flogged," Fouche said calmly. "He'll swing from the gallows by morning."

As a pair of guards dragged the now screaming wretch away, a third guard jammed the butt of his musket into the man's stomach, causing him to nearly vomit. He continued to curse both Fouche, as well as the king, as he was dragged down the side hall towards an interrogation room.

"Now then," the minister of police continued, "what about the rest of you?"

"What would you have us do?" a man who'd been convicted of both robbery and at least three murders asked. He was a horrid sight; one eye was missing, hideous scars covering his face. His left hand was missing two fingers, and what teeth he did have were mostly yellow and blackened. He knew he deserved to hang, yet he lustily eyed the king's chance at parole. His own execution was set to take place in two days, and now, just the chance of seeing the sun once more and breathing the air of a free man consumed him.

"Only what all of you are good at," Fouche replied. "There is an escaped traitor that the king needs disposed of, discreetly I might add."

"Who is he?" another robber asked.

"That is not your concern," Foss spoke up. "I will give you a detailed description of the man. Trust me, he will be easy to spot."

"Once you have eliminated this man, send word directly to my office," Fouche continued. "I will send a man to ascertain proof the deed has been done. Once finished, you will all be given the king's royal pardon, along with a generous donative of five hundred francs. You can then live your lives as men, rather than murderers and thieves."

"Where will we find this man?" the first criminal asked.

Just then they heard sounds of screaming down the hall, accompanied by the cracking of whips. Neither Fouche nor his deputy paid it any mind.

"He will head directly for the sea," Foss explained. "Rochefort is his most likely destination. We will have fast horses ready for you, along with both sabres and pistols."

"Know this," Fouche added, his majesty is being very magnanimous; where each of you deserves death tenfold, he is offering you both pardon and a generous amount of coin. Play him false, or fail in your mission, and you will all be drawn and quartered. My deputy will be following you, along with a score of my own men, both to support you and to ensure you do not fail."

Aglae's mind and body were both completely numb; all she could feel was the stabbing pain in her heart. She was dressed in mourning garb, a black veil blowing in the wind as she clenched her hands in frustration and sorrow. Her eldest son, Joseph, was not with her, for he had found a viable second to face the Duke of Wellington in the proposed duel. Aglae felt violently ill at the thought of another innocent having to die this day, for the young man who had bravely stepped forward to help her son defend the family's honour would surely be killed if the duel was allowed to proceed.

"Is it not enough that I have lost my husband?" she said, wiping away the tears that refused to be held back.

"But you haven't lost your husband," a voice said behind her.

Aglae turned, and upon the sight of Ida Sainte-Elme, her sorrow turned to anger.

"And what are *you* doing here?" she snapped. "You who lusted after my dear husband for years, like an unrepentant whore! Will you now mock his widow before his body is even laid into the ground?"

"Please hear me out," Ida said, holding her hands up in emphasis. "Your husband is not dead."

"Liar!" Aglae said, her voice dripping with venom.

"She speaks the truth, my child," Sister Therese said, as she walked around the corner. She bowed slightly. "Please forgive my late intrusion. I had to make certain there were no unfriendly ears listening."

"Sister," Aglae replied, softening her voice. She knew Therese or, at least, was acquainted with her. They had only met in passing a few times, yet Madame Ney had always respected her for the dignity she gave to the dead, regardless of what type of person they had been in life. "Please…please explain."

"God has found another purpose for your husband," the sister explained. "I cannot say what that purpose is, but know that Marshal Ney did not die by the muskets of the firing squad."

"How?"

"Let us just say, he found the unlikeliest of allies," Ida said.

"Wellington?" Aglae asked, suddenly understanding. "My God…Joseph!"

"It's alright," Ida said once more. "I have spoken to Wellington. He never had any intention of allowing the duel to proceed. The brave, albeit foolish, young man who stepped in for your son will not need to die this day."

"And Michel?" Relieved for the moment, Aglae's thoughts turned to her husband once more.

"I must return to him," Sister Therese said, "so we can get him out of Paris. After that, the matter will be in God's hands."

Ney knew he could not get out of Paris soon enough. He had watched from behind a window curtain as the cart bearing his casket was wheeled out into the main courtyard of the hospice. A few gendarmes were on hand to keep the crowds back as the wagon was hitched to a single mule.

"I didn't even rate a horse-drawn carriage," Ney quietly scoffed.

There was haste being made to place the coffin in the ground, lest word reached the king's ministers and they managed to open it and see it was devoid of a body. The gendarmes who now stood on either side of the wagon were clearly oblivious to the conspiracy, yet Michel knew it was only a matter of time before someone discovered the treachery.

"Once the coffin is in the ground, no one will dare disturb it," Sister Therese said, over his shoulder. She then told him, "Forgive me for my absence, but I had to go see your wife."

"Aglae," Ney said, turning to face her. "I must see her!"

"Not if you wish to continue living," the sister replied, shaking her head. "Though I was able to speak with her, and to let her know you lived, I know we were being watched. As the matron of this hospice, my going to see her would not raise any concerns. However, know that for some time, Madame Aglae will be watched by the minister of police's men."

"Vile bastards," the marshal snarled.

"Come, my son," Therese said, taking him by the arm. "It is time for you to leave this place of death. Take this gift of life renewed, which God Himself has given you, and use it for the benefit of His people."

On the table, where he had lain just recently, was his greatcoat and top hat, along with a sword and a loaded flintlock pistol, courtesy of General Sir Robert Wilson. In a leather pouch were a dozen cartridges for the weapon.

"There is food and water in the saddlebags," the sister said, as Michel scabbarded the sword and placed the pistol in his belt. "A certain 'friend' of yours was also able to procure a substantial portion of your personal wealth. Not to worry, your wife and children will want for nothing, though suffice it to say that it should be more than enough to allow you to live comfortably in the New World."

The marshal nodded, and in a move that completely surprised Sister Therese, he leaned forward and kissed her on the cheek.

"I thank you, sister," he said, throwing on his overcoat. "May God be as kind to you as He has been generous to me."

"One last thing," the sister said, her face blushing from the gesture shown by the marshal. She then handed him an envelope. "These are orders from the Duke of Wellington. His soldiers to give you safe passage and protection if need be. Redcoats patrol every city from here to Rochefort, so I have no doubt you will be needing this. It will guard you better than any weapon."

The courtyard was completely empty when Ney stepped out the front door to the hospice. It was far more inconspicuous for him to leave out the front, rather than trying to sneak out a side or back alley. Any who did see him would assume he was a worker at the hospice and pay him no mind. The chill of the December evening made his keeping the collar of his great coat up, with a scarf around his face, less noticeable. As he led his horse onto the streets, they were crowded with the ever-present mass of humanity as is such in a huge city. While the mob gave him a great deal of concealment, he shuddered every time he saw passing gendarmes or soldiers. At the bridge crossing that led to the suburb of Villeneuve-Saint-Georges, he saw a group of British soldiers checking travellers.

"Hold here," a private said, raising his hand. There were a dozen of them, and three were now focused on the mysterious man with the scarf and top hat, while their companions searched a wagon bearing grain. Ney knew there was nothing he could do as one of the men searched his saddle bags. The first soldier then said, "Put your arms up, please."

The marshal did as he was told, and one of the men quickly saw his pistol and sword.

"It is dangerous to be on the roads," Ney said, attempting to sound calm. "If you will check my left coat pocket, there is a document that gives me safe passage through your checkpoints."

The first soldier nodded to one of his companions, who started rooting through Ney's coat. He found the envelope, which he handed over, while continuing to check the rest of the pockets. Since all of the soldiers were privates, Ney suspected the one giving directives must have been the only one who could read. That soldier's eyes grew wide as he read the note.

"Let him go," he said quickly, handing the envelope back to Ney. He shouted to the other soldiers, "Clear a path! Let his man through!" There were hundreds of people and carriages crowded onto the bridge, all of whom started shouting protests and profanities towards both Ney and the soldiers.

"Hey, what the bleeding hell gives?" one of the soldiers asked, irritated. "Do you know what I found in his saddlebags?"

"Whatever it is, you'd best leave it alone and shut the hell up about it!" the first soldier retorted. "This man has travel documents signed by Old Nosey himself. So unless you want to explain to the Duke why his charge was delayed, I'd suggest we clear the fucking bridge!" A lane was soon mostly cleared as both wagons and people were roughly shoved to the side. One of the redcoats quickly waved the marshal through.

Ney touched his hat and led his horse through the crowd, mounting as soon as he was on the other side. As he rode away, one of the soldiers asked, "Who the bloody hell was that?"

"I have no idea," the man who'd read the documents replied. "But if he's got safe passage orders signed by Our Atty, I'd rather not be the poor sod who delays him."

It was well after dark by the time Ney cleared the Paris suburbs. Along the way, he ran into at least two more British checkpoints, though the soldiers at these had simply waved him through without bothering to search him. Knowing his pursuers would not be far behind, he rode all through the night until he reached the city of Orleans. Fearing he might be recognized if he went into an inn, where he'd be compelled to remove his hat and scarf, he found a grove of apple trees outside the city. While his horse picked some of the rotten fruit off the ground, Ney sat down at the base of a tree, wrapped in his great coat. His leaned his sword against the tree and rested his pistol in his lap. Despite his rattled nerves, as well as shivering from the damp cold, he allowed himself the first hours of sleep to come since his 'death'.

Back in Paris, no one except the king, Fouche, and a small number of others knew about the botched execution of Marshal Ney. As it was, there had been an unforeseen amount of extreme backlash brought on by his death. Though the peers, and even some of his fellow marshals, cared little for his demise, the common people openly mourned in the streets. To the poor and working class, it mattered little if he had served King Louis or Emperor Napoleon; to them, Marshal Ney had fought for France. Even a large number of royalists were now proclaiming it had been wrong to kill such a brave man. There would also come a biting rebuke from the British government in the coming weeks, which would greatly diminish King Louis' standing with his foreign allies.

Even in the Chamber of Peers, voices that had before remained silent out of fear for their own persons were suddenly finding their courage to speak out. One of these was General Exelmans, who had commanded the II Cavalry Corps at Waterloo. Though no long a Peer of France, having been among those stripped by the king after the Second Restoration, he was granted an audience in the Chambers with the aid of the Duke of Broglie.

*"The Chambers will now recognize General of Division Rémi Joseph Isidore Exelmans,"* the speaker announced.

"Thank you, mister speaker," Exelmans said, as he stepped up to the platform.

"For what reason do you wish to address this body?" the Duc de Noailles asked.

"To speak out regarding a wrong committed by the peers of France," the general said plainly. "I speak of course about the most recent execution of Michel Ney, Marshal of France."

His remark led to a hundred conversations beginning at once, with some shouting rebukes towards the general.

"It is not for you to question sentencing passed by this body!" Noailles snapped. "You should be held in contempt for insinuating as much!"

"General Exelmans is here on my authority," Broglie shot back. "He is a hero of France, who has distinguished himself in more battles than most of this body combined! It would be undignified if we held in contempt one who has served valiantly for so many years. The general will be allowed to speak!"

Noailles took his seat and said no more, nor did anyone else in the Chambers. Whatever General Exelmans said, it mattered little. Even though many within the Chambers were suddenly having a change of heart, there was nothing that could take back what had been done."

The speaker nodded to Exelmans, who took a deep breath before unleashing the verbal assault that had been building up within him ever since his friend's capture.

"The illegal sentencing and execution of Marshal Ney is an atrocity, one committed by this formerly august body!" he shouted angrily.

The members of the Chambers sat in eerie silence as Exelmans' furious words echoed. Whereas, a week before there were voracious cries of condemnation and demands for Ney's blood, there was suddenly shamed silence. "All of you, whether by convicting or abstaining, are guilty of a most abominable assassination! I spit on the Chambers, ashamed as I am to continue in service of, and therefore go into self-imposed exile in Nassau."

There were others who issued damning words against both King Louis and the Chamber of Peers. Most of the other Napoleonic marshals that had been convicted of treason had simply been exiled, with some like Marshal Grouchy actually acquitted. The king was now in an awkward position, for while he had completely misjudged the public reaction to Marshal Ney's execution, how would they react if it became known that their king was once again betrayed and the marshal still lived? He reasoned that anger over the execution would die down soon enough, but the humiliation of it being faked would undermine his already fragile authority greatly. No, there was no other path that could be followed now; Marshal Ney *had* to die. If he escaped from France, there would ever be the threat that he could surface once more to humiliate the Bourbons.

In the park known as *Bois de Boulogne*, the Duke of Wellington was finishing one last issue with the Ney family. He stood in his long frock coat, a flintlock pistol in his hand. Looking rather nervous stood a local magistrate, who held the box that had contained the pistols. As Joseph Ney was underage, he could not take part in a duel and, as such, a young French officer had agreed to stand in his place. The young man was scarcely old enough to shave, let alone hold a commission, and had never seen active service. He stood erect, yet was clearly terrified at facing down the venerable man who had bested Napoleon in battle. He was, however, willing to assist Marshal Ney's family in maintaining their honour, even though it would likely mean his death.

"You demand satisfaction for the death of your father," Wellington said calmly to young Joseph.

"Yes, sir," the boy replied. "I do, sir!"

"Then you will force me to kill once more," the duke stated as he half-cocked the pistol. "Know this, if you insist on satisfaction, a man will die on this field, but it will not be the Duke of Wellington."

Joseph swallowed hard, unsure as to what should be said.

The young officer's hand was trembling with absolute fear; even if he could get his shot off, there was no chance of it striking home, whereas the Duke's hand remained absolutely steady. He would not miss.

"Please, your grace!" the magistrate pleaded. "Accepting a challenge from a mere boy, it is unacceptable…"

"It is a matter of his family's dignity," the duke interupted, raising his hand to silence the man. He then addressed Joseph again, "I advise you to make certain your father's execution should warrant the death of another, lest this man, who has been good enough to come forward in your stead, should die for nothing."

All three were at a complete loss for words; young Joseph, the magistrate, as well as the extremely nervous officer. Wellington was cold and confident in his words, which bit as sharply as the frigid air of the early December morning. The was no doubt in the Duke's demeanour that he would walk away from the duel alive. What assailed Joseph was the understanding that if he persisted, the noble officer who stepped forward to defend his family would most certainly be killed.

"I..." he stammered. "I cannot ask this good man to die in vain. The family Ney must remain without satisfaction." He looked down, ashamed.

Wellington strode forward, handing the pistol back to the relieved magistrate, before waving for him and the officer to leave. He looked down at young Joseph. Having inherited his father's height, at twelve years of age he could almost look the Duke in the eye.

"Know this," Wellington said. "There is no dishonour in the name of Ney. The shame belongs to those who once called him friend, yet who later demanded his death. And understand one last thing; for your father, death was just the beginnning."

# Chapter XVIII: A Return to the Past

Cleveland, North Carolina
February, 1846
\*\*\*

A letter came to Alexander Reille as he finished his work for the day. Since graduating from Davidson College, he had found work as a tutor for the large number of French immigrants to whom he taught English and other skills. Many were former soldiers, or their families, who had no future in post-Napoleonic France. It was a noble undertaking, though the pay was less than substantial. Alexander's position was a private undertaking, and he received only that compensation which his pupils could afford to pay him. And since most needed to improve their English in order to make a viable living wage, there was little they could give in the way of compensation. Though he was quite passionate about helping the French immigrants succeed in their new country, he needed to find a profession that offered a more reliable wage. He was, therefore, applying to several colleges in Massachusetts, where he hoped his schooling and language abilities could aid him in earning a faculty position. The letter he had just received from Peter Stuart Ney would delay this for at least a little while.

Alexander was worried about his old schoolmaster, whom he now called 'friend'. They had stayed in contact over the last few years, with the ever-eclectic Frenchman promising the young man that he would soon be in great need of his services. With a sudden downturn in his health, it seemed that time had, at last, come. Peter Ney had always possessed a rather robust constitution, never so much as walking with a cane or needing assistance when mounting his horse, despite now being seventy-seven years of age. However, a rather brutal bout of pneumonia over the winter had weakened him considerably, and though he promised his friends he was on the mend, Alexander knew his teacher and mentor was not long for this world.

Now, well into his retirement years, Peter lived in a two-story colonial home that dated from prior to the American Revolution. Though far from ostentatious, its expense was clearly more than what a schoolmaster could afford, adding to the speculation that Peter had come to America with a substantial amount of money already in his possession.

The letter Alexander received had been rather vague, only stating that his former teacher needed him to perform a service that would involve his being away for an extended period. His curiosity sufficiently piqued, the young man decided that a faculty posting would have to wait for another day.

It was evening by the time the coach dropped Alexander off in front of his old schoolmaster's house. The black clouds made the sky dark, as if it were already night, with a few drops of rain and a flash of lightening foreboding the coming of a bad storm.

As he stood on the wrap-around porch and knocked on the door, Alexander noted the American and French flags that both blew in the stiff breeze from the front of the house. The door was opened by a black servant which, at first, surprised Alexander. Peter had lived alone since coming to the United States, though at his advanced age it should only be expected he would require help with his daily routine. Alexander also surmised that, given the Frenchman's absolute loathing of slavery, the man who answered the door was not a slave but a paid employee.

"Can I help you, sir?" the servant asked.

"I am here to see Mister Ney. Tell him it's Alexander Reille."

"Ah, of course," the older man said with a smile. "He has been expecting you these past few days. Please, do come in."

As the flash of lightning and subsequent crash of thunder echoed outside, there was a sudden downpour of rain that echoed loudly off the roof and walls of the house. The servant seemed nonplussed, having spent most of his life in North Carolina. He held aloft an oil lamp and guided Alexander towards a study at the back of the house.

"Alexander Reille to see you, sir," the servant said.

"Alexander!" Peter said enthusiastically, as he stood up from his thick leather armchair. Though he now walked with a cane, he still stood erect, like the old soldier that he was. He then nodded to the servant. "Thank you, Jonathan."

The old schoolteacher waved Alexander over to another large armchair across from his own. Off to the side, in between, was a small end table with a lamp and some books.

"It is good you have come," Peter said, leaning back in his chair. The young man noticed a slight tremble in his hand that wasn't there before, as well as a sagging in his left eye, as if he were constantly fatigued. "I have need of you, as you gathered from my letter. I hope it is not a grave inconvenience for you."

"I was intending to move up to Boston in search of a position at Becker College, or perhaps even Boston University," Alexander replied. "But those can wait."

"Well, the last thing I wish to do is to keep you from pursuing your dreams," the old man said as he tried to sit upright.

"Dreams…no," Alexander said with a shaking of his head. "While I do hope to find at least an adjunct professor position, it is still just a job. A dream for me would be to see the land of your birth. France, and indeed, all of Europe has held immense interest for me since my earliest schooldays, when you used to tell us of all the history there; thousands of years of civilization to be explored! It is something we simply do not have here."

"America will have to make its own history," Peter noted. He smiled. "But I am glad you share such an interest in my country, for I miss it dearly. Every day I dream of returning home, but sadly it was never meant to be. It is you, my friend, who must go in my stead." He stood slowly and walked over to an oak desk, where another oil lamp burned dimly.

"Here," he said, pulling out a pair of envelopes from the top drawer. "I suppose I could just send these through the post, but I want assurance that they reach their intended recipients. Besides, there are some documents I wish for you to retrieve from the first address."

"Of course," the young man replied. He read the first envelope, which was the much thicker of the two. "To Madame Aglae Ney." He scrunched his brow in thought. "Wasn't that the name of the famous marshal's wife?"

"There are a number of French women named Aglae," Peter replied dismissively. "Just as there are other families with the surname of Ney. That there would be more than one woman in all of France to bear both names is hardly surprising."

Alexander grinned knowingly. Peter had gone out of his way to sound dismissive, rather than simply answering the question. Of course, this in itself meant nothing unusual, though it did give the young man pause, especially after some of the stories he'd heard about the famous Marshal of France. He remembered back to his school days, when he'd seen a portrait of Marshal Ney, or rather a sketching done of the original. He had said, at the time, that it bore a striking resemblance to his teacher. Peter had chuckled and said with a wink, "Yes, perhaps he's a relative."

"The address should still be valid," the old man added. "And if not, people will know where to find her if, in fact, she still lives. Sadly, I know not for certain."

Alexander did not inquire further, but instead read the other envelope.

"To Field Marshal Sir Arthur Wellesley, Duke of Wellington," he read aloud. "Address: Number One, London."

"Yes, it is not just to France that I need you to go," Peter explained. "You must also go to the city of a people who were once my enemies…and yours for that matter."

"The last time we fought the British was around the time I was born," Alexander said. "That was a hateful affair, which benefited no one, except perhaps the arms manufacturers."

"War has always brought sorrow and destruction to many, while a select few profit immensely," Peter noted. "There are those, I'm afraid, who would keep the world in a perpetual state of war, just so that they can continue to fill their coffers. A wretched lot they are!"

Alexander found the rather damning rebuke towards the arms manufacturing industry a bit confusing, especially given Peter's former life as a soldier. Rather than pursuing the matter further, he returned to the reason for his visit. It was a bit surreal to him, that his old friend was asking him to actually travel to Europe on his behalf.

"London is a city I have longed to visit," he said, "as much as Paris, to be honest. I am curious, though, as to your relationship with the Duke of Wellington."

"Let us just say he was once my greatest enemy," the old French soldier remarked. "And yet, of everyone from my past life—which was so long ago it does not seem real to me some days—in the end he was, perhaps, my only friend."

Peter had compensated Alexander quite handsomely for his service, having given the young man a thousand dollars upfront with which to travel and to cover any necessary expenses. Alexander had tried to protest, stating that even if he were gone a year, it would only cost a fraction of what he was given. Peter would hear none of it, only adding that there would be another four thousand waiting in his bank account when he returned. Such a sum would allow Alexander to live quite comfortably for a very long time, and while it made him slightly embarrassed to accept, he knew it would be very poor manners to refuse his former teacher's extreme generosity.

A few letters were hastily written to a couple of family members and friends, letting them know he would be away for a number of months, before booking passage to 'The Old World'. With no ships in North Carolina headed anywhere near France, Alexander first had to make his way to Norfolk, Virginia; a trip by carriage that took nearly two weeks. Once he arrived, he spent a few days waiting on a ship that was headed for France. Once he found a suitable vessel, for a few extra dollars he was able to purchase a small cabin aboard a cargo ship that was transporting cotton to Bordeaux.

Alexander had never travelled by sea, and he was immediately sick before the ship had even pulled out of the harbour. He was grateful for having his own cabin, for he could hang his head from the window, the crew not having to witness his shame as he heaved violently until long after the contents of his stomach had been completely expelled. Little did the young man know, seasickness was as common as the day was long, and most were stricken as he was upon their first voyage.

A week passed before his stomach allowed him to eat. He found that the air of the top deck was quite refreshing, though he was required to make certain he stayed out of the crew's way. The journey by sea was tedious, lasting nearly a month. Just when he was thinking they would never reach the shores of France, a lookout shouted that land had been sighted. Bordeaux port was deceptively farther away than it appeared, and while Alexander was ecstatic to finally be arriving, it was several hours from the time of the sighting before they finally docked in the vast harbour.

He gathered up his belongings, thanked the captain for his hospitality, and set about finding lodgings for the night. He was then grateful for all of the French lessons Peter Ney had given him, and that he had continued his language studies at Davidson College. His first night in France would consist of little more than finding an inn, along with some supper, before bedding down for the night. From his bedroom window he could hear the sounds of the seas, as well as the ships in the harbour. In the morning, he would start on the mysterious journey his teacher had sent him on. As he drifted off, his old suspicions about who Peter Stuart Ney was consumed his subconscious.

# Chapter XIX: A Bloody Escape

Between Orleans and Poitiers, France
10 December 1815

Corporal and Private, Grenadier Guards

A very brief update to their orders had reached Corporal Shepard and his riflemen three days prior, letting them know that a horrific storm had felled a number of trees and blown a great many obstacles onto the roads. This meant that most wheeled traffic headed through Poitiers was being diverted to alternate routes for the time being. It also meant their quarry would be easier to spot, as would any assailants in pursuit. Several had passed their way, though none had matched the description the major had given them.

"Rider approaching, corporal!" a rifleman said, shaking Martin and awakening him from his fitful slumber.

The NCO had been up most of the night, and had only managed a few minutes of sleep after each approaching rider was shown not to be who they were looking for. Martin wiped his eyes and slapped himself across the face to try and wake up. He then took a long pull off his water bladder before crawling over to where the soldier who had woken him lay prone, behind a soaked and rotting log.

"Can't see a fucking thing," the rifleman grumbled as he wiped a rag over his pocket telescope. "Blasted mist is obscuring everything down there…and this damn thing keeps fogging up!"

"Calm yourself, man," Martin chastised, as he wiped down his own glass before scanning the road below. It was, indeed, quite misty, and his telescope, likewise, kept fogging every few seconds. Still, he was able to make out the features of the man who now guided his horse towards them along the saturated road. Trees and limbs from the recent storm littered the path, and he was now leading his horse through the mess.

"Black top hat," he observed. "Judging by his height when compared to his mount, I would reckon he's quite tall. What colour would you say his hair is?"

"Looks coppery to me," the rifleman replied, before wiping off his scope once more.

"That's our man," the corporal said, noting for himself the red hair atop the man's head. He then told the soldier, "Go back and inform the rest of the lads. Have them take up their positions past the far bend in the road. If they hear shots from us, they'll know our friend is in trouble."

"Yes, corporal," the private said, picking up his rifle and running as fast as he could through the dense undergrowth back to where Martin had posted two of his two-man teams. His remaining were split into two pairs, one on each side of the road.

Martin continued to scan the path and the thick undergrowth as the rider led his horse through the fallen trees and branches. A flash in the thicket behind the rider alerted him; a slight delay coming from the time he spotted the muzzle flash reflected in the mist, to when he heard the report of the pistol shot. The assailants had not only fired too soon, for the rider was well beyond the range of the weapon, but it had also alerted him to their presence. And what neither the rider nor his would-be assassins knew was that a team of Britain's best marksmen lay hidden along both hills the road ran between.

As his rifleman returned and fell down beside him, Corporal Shepard rested his Baker Rifle on the log, looking down his sights towards where the shot had come from. The shape of a dark blur in the mist told him of a man who still sat astride his horse as he negotiated the fallen obstacles. Martin cocked his weapon, took a deep breath which he exhaled halfway, as he quickly did a final estimate on the range to his target, aligned his sights, and gently squeezed the trigger.

The crack of a pistol shot echoed just behind Ney. Luckily, it went wide and splintered a nearby fallen tree. The marshal looked back to see at least six men in the shadows of the mist. They were mounted and trying to site their pistols at him. They had misjudged the distance and were firing at him well beyond the range of a flintlock pistol. Ney first thought to draw his own sidearm, but realizing one shot against half a dozen men would prove futile, he instead mounted his horse and continued to ride through the mass of fallen branches and dead trees.

As soon as he reached a clear stretch of road, he heard another loud shot; but this one had come from his front, not from behind. It was also much louder than a pistol, and echoed as the sound bounced around the hillsides. A voice from the mist screamed and Ney glanced back long enough to see one of the assassins fall from his horse. He was hit in the shoulder, and he continued to shriek in pain as he thrashed about.

As he kicked his horse into a canter, Ney saw the flash of another weapon and was able to make out a pair of men in green and black jackets, wielding what he could only assume were Baker rifles. Whether these men were dispatched by Wellington to protect him, or just soldiers tasked with keeping an eye out for bandits, it mattered not. Although, if King Louis' men were getting more desperate in their attempts to finish him, then so were Wellington's soldiers in their efforts to save him.

With the report of a second rifle, another one of Ney's attackers fell screaming from his horse. During the Peninsular War, and later at Waterloo, the marshal had grown to hate the men in the green jackets, for their weapons had a far greater range and accuracy than any of the French skirmishers. Their presence on the battlefield always led to a disproportionate number of casualties among the officers and NCOs who were specifically targeted by the riflemen. Ney gritted his teeth at the irony, that some of the very men who had likely tried to kill him on numerous occasions were now coming to his aid. He spurred his horse into a full gallop as two more rifle shots rang out.

Two men lay sprawled on the road; one thrashing about with a shattered shoulder that was bleeding profusely, the other dead from a shot through the lungs. Four more men had ridden through the ambush, and although Corporal Shepard and his men prided themselves on their superior marksmanship, even soldiers of the 95$^{th}$ Rifles struggled to hit a moving target at such long range. Just as the NCO finished ramming the ball home as he reloaded his rifle, a series of shots rang out from just up the road. The bandits had run into the rest of his section.

"Come on!" he shouted, waving his men to follow him. He stumbled and slipped down the slope of slick grass and scrub brush and onto the road.

Surprise was gone, and there was no point in remaining concealed any further. He tasked two of his men to keep a rear guard and watch for any other riders that may be coming up the road, while he and his remaining rifleman sprinted towards the sound of gunfire.

The sound of galloping horses alerted him, and he raised his hand, halting his men. The four men stood in line with each other, rifles at the ready.

"They're coming back!" Martin shouted. He quickly dropped down to one knee, his men following his lead.

He soon saw three of the riders racing back towards them. One held his hand over his stomach and was slouched forward in the saddle.

His riflemen did not wait for any subsequent orders. Each rested his support elbow on his forward leg and carefully sighted down their weapons towards their rushing enemy. It was not the first time any of them had faced the charge of enemy horsemen, although the last time they had done so, it had been entire regiments of French hussars, along with the fearsome armoured cuirassiers. Three mounted robbers, one of whom was already badly injured, posed no threat to them. They allowed the riders to close the distance, in order to ensure greater accuracy. Just as one of the assassins drew his pistol, Martin felled him with a shot straight through the heart. The other two riders were knocked from their horses; the wounded man taking a rifle ball through the face, which exploded out the back of his head.

"*Rifles, up!*" Martin shouted down the road.

The remaining four men of his section were soon seen running up the road towards them.

"We got the last one, corporal," one of the men said, panting as he was out of breath. "Our Atty's friend made it through safely."

"Good work," Martin replied. He then nodded towards the bodies. "These three have bought it, we left one more dead and one badly wounded back up the road. What of their friend?"

"Gut shot," the rifleman replied. "He'll not be long for this world. We started to interrogate him before you called to us, but all he would do is scream and thrash about like a two-guinea whore."

"Hmm, well, let us see if we can get any useful information out of the other one," the corporal said.

"Like who in the bloody piss that is they was chasing," one of his men scoffed.

"Yeah, it would be great to get a little insight into at least one of Old Nosey's little secrets," another bantered as they walked back up the road, having collected three of the bandits' horses.

As they reached the thickets, where they first engaged the robbers, they saw the first man sprawled on his back, his good arm out to his side with his smoking pistol lying next to it. The side of his head was blown away, his eyes wide and lifeless.

"Well, shit," Martin grumbled. "Looks like we won't be getting any useful intelligence from these bastards. Check their saddlebags for anything of use. I'll take one of the horses back to Poitiers and inform the lieutenant."

It would be well after dark by the time Corporal Shepard reached Poitiers, by which time it had started to rain once more. To make matters worse, he had left his greatcoat at the camp. He was starting to think that following in his grandfather's footsteps and becoming a butler was not such a bad choice of profession after all.

Ney did not know if his pursuers were still behind him. A second volley of gunfire had erupted soon after the first, and he spurred his horse into a full sprint. A subsequent volley echoed not long after this, though it was quite some distance behind him. After about a mile he slowed his horse and chanced a glance back behind his shoulder. The path was clear, and the marshal could only assume that either the English soldiers had killed or captured his attackers or else they had fled. He slowed to an easy trot as he continued on his way. What neither he nor the British soldiers knew was that a pair of assassins had taken a lesser known path and made their way around the checkpoint, in an attempt to catch the marshal in a trap of their own.

The shot of a pistol caused Ney's horse to rear up, throwing him off. As he landed hard onto the damp road, the wind was knocked from him for a brief moment. He rolled to his left, a pain shooting through his side as he tried to stagger to his feet.

Two men came crashing out of the thick undergrowth, both in dark cloaks with tricorn hats. One still carried a pistol that was smoking from the barrel; the other's firearm was still tucked into his belt. Both men now had their swords drawn and were walking briskly towards him. Realizing he had only a few seconds, Ney elected to remain on his back, as the ground would provide a stable platform for him to fire from. He quickly pulled the pistol General Wilson had given him from his belt and aimed for the brigand who still had a loaded weapon. A number of distressing thoughts went through the marshal's mind as he cocked the hammer back: Was it loaded properly? Had the rains dampened the powder in the flash pan? Would he be able to get to his feet in time before the second attacker either retrieved his friend's pistol or ran him through with his sword?

Ney exhaled slowly, keeping his composure as he squeezed the trigger. Even in the most capable of hands, the flintlock pistol had a notoriously short effective range; yet the powder ignited and with a loud crack the shot flew from the end of the muzzle, and Ney saw his intended target double over. The man screamed in agony as the ball slammed into his stomach.

Knowing he'd been shot, he rolled onto his non-injured side and up to his feet, drawing his sword in the process. He placed his left hand where the wound was. It was painful to touch and seeping blood, though it was not impeding his ability to breathe.

"Come," he said as he settled into his fighting stance, his weapon pointing towards his foe. "You've already wounded me, now finish the king's bidding, if you dare."

That his voice was very calm, as if he were having a casual conversation, unnerved his attacker. He had shot the marshal, and yet here he stood, ready for battle! There would be no time to reload his pistol, nor could he possibly retrieve the sidearm of his fallen companion, who groaned in agony as he slowly expired. Having no other options, he drew his own blade and rushed his adversary.

Marshal Ney was a master swordsman, having been trained in the art since he was very young. He quickly parried the assassin's thrust, while blocking several follow-on slashes. Ney was acting purely defensively for the moment, learning his opponent's strengths and weaknesses before attacking. He eyed the man's feet, noting that they were almost never under him as he lunged forward time and again nor did he attempt to strike with any kind of precision. The marshal knew immediately that his adversary was an amateur with no formal training with a sword. He let the man make one last mistake, driving forward with a lunging thrust that left him off-balance. Ney brought his own blade down in a hard chop, slashing the man's forearm and causing him to drop his weapon. Before he could even yelp in pain, Ney had the point of his sword pressed into the flesh of his chest. The marshal raised the hilt of his weapon, causing his attacker to drop to his knees. One quick thrust would end it.

"How many more of you are there?" Ney asked.

The man spat on the ground in response.

The marshal then added coldly, "I can do a lot more than just kill you now. I can make you suffer torments beyond your comprehension if you do not answer me."

"I don't know how many they've sent," the assassin said, shaking his head. "There was, perhaps, ten of us who left the gaol in Paris. Who knows how many more they later released. The minister of police said he would have men following us to make certain we did our job. They can't be too far behind." He then shook his head and spat on the ground once more. "A full pardon and five hundred francs they offered us. Lot of good it'll do me now."

"Serves Fouche right, sending such pathetic amateurs after me," Ney scoffed.

"You'd best finish me," the man said. He attempted to show defiance in his voice, yet Ney could sense the abject defeat in the man's face. He then added, "I'm a dead man anyway. Once Fouche hears of your escape, he'll have me hanged. But I'll be damned if I know who in the hell you are or why your death is worth paying us each five hundred francs!"

Ney nodded and made ready to drive his weapon through the man's heart when a voice shouted, *"Lâchez votre arme! Drop your weapon!"*

The marshal looked up to see six red-jacketed soldiers running towards him from up the road. The man who shouted at him had his musket raised up and aimed at Ney's head. The black facings on his uniform denoted he was from one of the elite Guards regiments, although his accent was a thick Irish brogue. And, though his boyish face gave away the fact that he was very young, probably not even twenty, he sported a pair of corporal's chevrons on his upper arm.

Ney raised his left hand up and slowly backed away, keeping the point of his sword brandished in front of his opponent. He then knelt down, placing the sword on the ground.

"That's it, nice and easy," the Irish corporal said as he stepped forward, his musket still aimed at the marshal. He was quickly joined by several of his mates, who had their weapons at waist height but aimed towards the men.

Hoping to finish the job he'd set out to do, the assassin drew an unseen dagger from the back of his belt and raised his arm up to throw it at Ney. The British corporal proved too quick, and he turned his musket on the man, firing a close range shot into the back of his head. His forehead exploded in a spray of blood, bone, and brain matter as the musket ball burst through.

"Exploded like a bloody pumpkin that did!" a redcoat laughed with macabre humour as the body of the bandit lay twitching, blood gushing from the gaping holes in his head.

"Search him, Private Farrow," the corporal directed, waving his musket towards Ney once more.

While the marshal stood with his hands up, the private proceeded to go through his pockets and pat him down. Ney grimaced as they roughly grabbed his injured side.

"Here, what do you make of this, David?" Farrow asked, pulling an envelope from Ney's pocket. It was clear the two men were close friends, for the corporal did not berate him for calling him his given name. The young NCO's eyes widened as he read the short message, his gaze fixed on the Duke's signature at the bottom.

"Bugger me," he said quietly. "It would seem this is the man of great importance to his grace we've been told to keep an eye out for. Alright, Farrow, let him be."

"David, he's been hit!" the private said quickly, as he opened the marshal's greatcoat. The undershirt was saturated with blood.

"Shit…" David swore, quickly pocketing the letter. He then waved to two of the other soldiers. "Help him!"

Ney's face was pale, and he was suddenly dizzy. Three sets of hands grabbed him under the arms and back as the soldiers helped him sit.

"Easy does it, sir," the corporal said, his tone completely changed from just a few moments before. He then shouted to one of the soldiers, "Fetch the surgeon! And inform Major Webster!"

The men laid the marshal back, his head resting on the knee of one of the soldiers. The corporal and another man tore open his undershirt, examining the wound.

"Think its hit anything vital?" the private asked.

"How in the bleeding fuck should I know?" the corporal retorted. "If I knew such things, I would be a sodden doctor."

"Extract the shot and keep me from bleeding to death, and I'll be fine," Ney said.

The soldiers were surprised not only by his flawless English, but that his voice was surprisingly calm.

"Bugger me," the corporal replied with a nervous laugh. "You've just been shot, sir, yet you're more composed than the rest of us."

James practically bounded out the front door to the inn, not even bothering to don his shako, as soon as he got word about the wounding of their charge. He gave his horse to Corporal Harvey, whom he sent to find the regimental surgeon. He ran up the road, Sergeant Donaldson and several others following, when he came upon Corporal O'Connor and his men helping the injured man. The first thing the major noticed was just how tall he was. Despite lying on his back, with his head propped up by one of his soldiers, James could tell he stood at least half a foot taller than any of his men. His thick, ginger-coloured hair also stood out conspicuously.

"Damn it all," the major said quietly.

# Chapter XX: Lady of France

Paris, France
March, 1846

Grave where Marshal Ney was reinterred in 1903
Père Lachaise Cemetery, Paris

The first thing that stood out to Alexander as he journeyed through France was just how old everything was. Many of the buildings, from the houses, to shops, to the chateaus and castles, dated from long before the first explorers had landed in North America. The country was also much drier than he anticipated. As he left Bordeaux, he heard locals say that they were in a drought and it looked like 1846 would be a bad year for crops. This did not bode well for the poor and working class. Any food shortages brought on by a lacklustre harvest would drive up inflation and lead to starvation amongst France's most humble subjects.

And, though the Bourbons had been overthrown in the *July Revolution of 1830*, the current king, Louis Philippe, was extremely unpopular. It was not always this way, a rider in the coach told him. Louis-Philippe had been called the 'Citizen King' early in his reign, while avoiding the pomp and excesses of the Bourbons. He had even ordered Napoleon's remains to be returned to France. Despite these deeds, as well as the general consensus that the king was a good man, he simply could not maintain the love of the people. Most of his support came from the wealthy *bourgeoisie*, while the king himself lived with unfortunate amalgam of being regarded as both royal and revolutionary. Whether truth or fantasy, the people's perception was that he was the very worst of both the Bourbons and the Bonapartists. There was even talk of trying to compel him to abdicate, with France becoming a republic once more. If, indeed, the drought brought on a food shortage that, in turn, spiralled into an economic crisis, it would be King Louis-Philippe who the people would hold responsible.

"A bit unfair, don't you think, to hold a king accountable for the actions of God?" Alexander asked. The man who sat across from him could only shrug.

"The people are fickle," he said. "The king is supposedly appointed by God, and if the Lord lets the people suffer, then his divine representative is who shoulders the blame…or something to that effect. Regardless, the people cannot exactly take out their grievances on God, yet they can on the king."

The young American found it all strange, never having lived in a nation that had a monarch. He thought how perverse it would be if Americans ever came to blame the president for all of their troubles. How absurd if a drought came to the United States and the people blamed it on President Polk!

The journey from Bordeaux to Paris took more than two weeks as Alexander hired various coaches, wagons, and in some cases, walked the three hundred and sixty-five miles through the French countryside. As he made his way through Poitiers and Orleans, he could not comprehend that thirty years before, these had been occupied by British redcoats following the fall of Napoleon. His instincts did tell him there was something even more significant about the path he followed to the French capitol, though he could not quite say what it was.

Arriving in Paris near midnight, Alexander found lodgings along the *Rue Belgrand*. From his room, his window overlooked a small block of houses, beyond which was an enormous cemetery, the *Père Lachaise*. As he undid his shirt and made ready for bed, Alexander knew there was something he had to do in the morning, before he went to pay a visit to Madame Ney.

Opened in 1804, the Père Lachaise Cemetery had among its more famous 'residents' were a number of Napoleon's generals and marshals; either those killed during the wars or who had since died after. There was one in particular whose grave Alexander simply had to see for himself.

The entrance was a large gate within a high stone wall. On either side were decorative columns, accented by stone torch, and in the centre was an hourglass with wings coming out of it. A series of stone wreaths donned the arch itself. As he walked through the cemetery, which was engulfed in tall trees, he found the *Chemin Massena,* or *Massena Path*. He followed this until he came upon a tomb in the shape of a pyramid on the left hand side. It was here he hoped to find what he was looking for, but it was not to be.

"Excusez-moi," he said to a passing young man. "Où puis-je trouver la tombe du Maréchal Ney?"

The man said nothing but simply signalled for Alexander to follow him. They left through the main entrance, with the Frenchman pointing to a narrow dirt path, just outside of the cemetery proper. Alexander walked along the weed-strewn trail until he came to a small cluster of graves in a very rundown burial site; for it did not fit the dignity of even being called a 'cemetery'. Many of the markers were worn from years of neglect and unreadable. However, he did find one that stood out as being far more recent than the others. Tucked away in a corner, covered with dead brambles, the tomb was really nothing more than a simple slab grave. Inscribed in the stone was: *Michel Ney, Duc d'Elchingen, Prince de la Moskowa.*

A chill ran up Alexander's spine. It was as if the cold stone was mocking him; like it knew what he had long suspected about his old schoolteacher, and now it was trying to crush that dream. Carved into the rock were words harshly stating that Michel Ney, Marshal of France, had died more than thirty years before. Though what it failed to note was that he had been shot as a traitor; unlawfully executed to placate the petty vengeance of a bitter monarch.

Alexander looked down at the stone slab covering the grave itself, adorned with a large simple crucifix. He cocked his head slightly as he gazed upon the grave and said quietly to himself, "An empty grave?"

The young American was feeling rather sombre as he left the cemetery and navigated the congested streets of Paris in search of Madame Aglae's residence. Located not far from the Palace of Versailles, from the outside it appeared to be rather a modest town home. When a servant opened the door for him, Alexander saw that it was quite ornate and spacious within. He was ushered into a small drawing room and, though offered a seat, he elected to remain standing. The walls were lined with old books, with several large portraits on the walls. One was of three very young boys, the other he could only assume was of Madame Ney herself. Her dark hair was worn up, with two rows of pearls atop, and another string of pearls around her neck. She wore a red dress with gold accents and what appeared to be a fur shawl.

"Il y a longtemps, c'était," a woman's voice said, stating the painting was from long ago.

Alexander turned to face her.

Aglae Ney was still a very striking woman. In her early to mid-sixties, the years had done little to lessen her beauty. Her once black hair was accented with grey in places. The lines of age around her face and eyes far less pronounced than one would expect.

"Bonne journée à vous, monsieur," Madame Ney added, wishing him a good day.

"Et...pour vous, Madame," he replied. "I bring a letter from my employer. He asked me to deliver it to you personally."

"Indeed," Aglae raised an eyebrow. "Who in America would have need to send a personal courier to me?" She opened the envelope and had just started to read the first page of the rather thick letter when she immediately stopped. Her face was pale, and Alexander thought perhaps she might faint. Instead, she closed the envelope and handed it to a servant. "Thank you, I shall read this later. May I offer you tea or coffee?"

"Coffee, thank you. There were also some documents he wished for me to retrieve." Alexander pulled out a list from his pocket.

Aglae looked it over. "I think I know where most of these are, though if they are not here, then they have most likely been lost. I'll have them brought down for you."

As he sat down, Alexander noticed a portrait of a soldier on campaign on the end table. The location wasn't clear, as the background was covered in snow, Alexander reckoned it might have been Russia. The man was very imposing, wearing a heavy greatcoat over his uniform, along with white trousers and black riding boots. A bicorn hat sat atop his head, and a sword was clasped in his right hand.

"Le brave des braves," Aglae said quietly, as she sipped her coffee.

"The bravest of the brave," Alexander translated. He looked her in the eye. "Your husband?"

Madame Ney nodded. "He fought a hundred battles for France. Yet, in the end, France betrayed him." Though the anger and bitterness had subsided over time, it was clear, even after thirty years, there was still an air of sadness about her.

"Not to intrude, Madame," Alexander said slowly, gaging his words carefully. "When I was in school, we learned about Marshal Ney and his undeserved fate. A lady friend of mine later asked why his wife never remarried."

"How could I remarry?" Aglae asked with a soft smile. "After all…" She immediately stopped herself short, as if she was about to spill a dark secret.

A silence followed as both drank their coffee, and Alexander stared at the portrait. Perhaps his mind was simply playing tricks on him, but even given the lack of finite detail in the picture—which he was certain was a replica of a much larger original—he could not help but notice a pronounced resemblance between the man pictured and his old schoolmaster. Peter had dismissively said one time that perhaps Marshal Ney was a relative, though from the portrait they looked as if they could be brothers, the same person even. As Peter Stuart Ney was a very old man now, Alexander tried to think back to when he first had the Frenchman as a teacher, and how he looked then. He also thought back to the grave he had just come from. Though it had dampened his spirits at the time, what was a grave anyway? It was a slab of stone and nothing more. Many graves, Marshal Murat's for example, were devoid of any mortal remains.

Alexander finally decided there was no sense in trying to be demure. He would likely never get a chance to speak with the wife of Marshal Ney again.

"Madame, there is something I must know. I just came from the grave of the good marshal, and yet from this picture, I could swear that the tomb lies empty. Forgive me if this is intrusive, but please tell me, who is Peter Stuart Ney? Is he the Marshal of France?"

A further silence followed, and Alexander could see that Aglae was fighting against a flood of memories. Her eyes had just started to water slightly, and he thought to apologise for his question, when she answered him.

"The Marshal of France," she said, "lies buried in Père Lachaise Cemetery. But if you want to know who Peter Stuart Ney is, I cannot answer that for you. But I promise you this, should you ask him who he is, whatever answer he gives you will be the truth."

Alexander thanked Madame Ney for her time, leaving as the late afternoon crowds filled the streets, the parcel of documents under his arm. He pulled up the collar on his long overcoat as he walked along the drizzly avenue. It was evening by the time he reached the inn, and while still quite busy, the crowds had thinned considerably.

That evening, as he sat in his room, curiosity got the best of him and he started to look through the parcel Madame Ney had given him. A lot of it appeared to be official reports, written by Marshal Ney during various campaigns. There was also a sketching of a man that was entitled, 'Ney by himself'. It was a simple charcoal drawing, showing the man, presumably Marshal Ney, leaning back against what could have been a couch, with his hand in the front of his jacket in a pose similar to that made famous by Napoleon.

He was now even more anxious to return to Cleveland, if for no other reason than he worried greatly about the health of his friend. Where once there had been such strength and vitality, the old teacher had appeared rather frail when he left. Alexander feared that Peter may be dead before they could speak again, and then there would be no way of answering the questions that still lingered within. Yet, as much as he wished to return home, his mission was not complete.

Before returning to America, he first had to make his way to England.

The French economy was slowly growing, in light of the Industrial Revolution. However, it still did not support nor justify a national rail system like the British. Therefore, while a train could conceivably take Alexander from Paris to Caen in a matter of hours, there was no direct line to the port city. The rail reached as far as Rouen, and while another line was being added to Le Havre, it was still at least a year from completion. Knowing he had few options, Alexander resolved to take the rail to Rouen, then attempt to hire a coach to take him to Caen. From there it would be a short trip across the channel into England.

Aglae held the curtain of the drawing room back just enough to watch the young American walk down the long walk and onto the main road. The young man's visit brought back a flood of memories, many of which had lain just beyond the fringe of conscious thought.

For more than thirty years Aglae had lingered in a perpetual state of mourning; a Purgotory of sorts. Her husband was gone, yet he still lived. She could not go to him nor could he ever return to her. In many ways, it was worse than if he had been killed all those years ago. At least then, there would have been a sense of closure!

More recently, there had been the unsubstantiated rumour that her third son, Eugene, had died the previous fall. This was brought on by loathesome gossips who assumed that, since they had not seen the young man in years, he must be dead. In fact, her son now lived in America, though it pained her when she learned that he had left the name of Ney behind. Was he ashamed of it, or did he simply wish to leave his family's past behind him? She did not know. Correspondance over such great distances could take months to reach the intended recipients, if it arrived at all. Perhaps that was why 'Peter' had used the young American as his personal courier instead of relying on the post.

Later that evening, Aglae pored through the pages of the letter under the soft glow of a small oil lamp. The last paragraph brought conflicting tears of both joy and sadness. She pressed her lips to the pages before rereading them one more time.

*...since God has deemed that we not be reunited in this world, then I look forward to the day when we meet again in Paradise. As you have waited all these years for me, so will I wait for you.*

# Chapter XXI: The Safety of Ones Enemies

### British Checkpoint South of Orleans
### 10 December 1815
### ***

The regimental surgeon arrived about an hour after Major Webster and his men brought the badly injured man to the inn. They laid him out in a private room at the top of the stairs, and while they had not attempted to remove the pistol shot, they had bandaged the wound enough to stop the bleeding.

"Let me see that," the surgeon said, as he pulled the bandage off the wound. "Yes…looks like it missed the vitals, though it's in there pretty deep. Lost a lot of blood, too."

"I've had worse," Ney said with a weak smile. His face was pale and his forehead damp.

The doctor retrieved his forceps from his bag and looked the marshal in the eye, who simply nodded.

"This is going to hurt," the surgeon said.

Ney grabbed onto the bed's mattress, his gaze fixed on the doctor as he probed the wound. Though his face twitched, the marshal made not a sound as the shot was extracted.

"There we are!" the surgeon said, as he produced the bloody pistol shot. "I'll be damned. Most men would have either cried out or fainted from such a wound. I'll need to clean it out before stitching you up."

Sergeant Donaldson brought up a wash basin full of hot water. The doctor took a clean rag, which he soaked in the steaming liquid before wiping away the filth and dried blood that had coagulated around the wound. He then proceeded to stitch the gouge in the marshal's side before wrapping a clean bandage around him.

Ney nodded in thanks before allowing himself to fall into a deep sleep. It was the first real slumber he'd had since his escape. It was a strange twist of fate that he was now safest, surrounded by armed soldiers who had once been his enemies.

"How is he?" James asked.

"He's lost a lot of blood," the surgeon replied. "But as long as the wound doesn't get infected, he'll live. What happened to him?"

"He was being chased by robbers," the major said. "He managed to kill one of them, the other was shot by one of my men."

"Hmm," the doctor mumbled. "Well, normally I would not recommend him moving about, least of all riding again, for at least a week, maybe two. That being said, he is one tough bastard." He then gathered up his instruments and bid the major good day.

"So who the devil is he, sir?" Sergeant Donaldson asked, soon after the doctor left.

They watched their sleeping charge, who was snoring quietly.

"Someone of great importance to Wellington," the major replied.

"Yes, but why?" Donaldson persisted.

"Since when has it ever been your place to comprehend what is important to his grace, sergeant?" James remarked sternly. "Ours is not to question why."

"Apologies, sir," Donaldson said. As he started to leave the room, he turned about and remarked, "Still is rather intriguing, though. I mean, judging from his size alone, he'd be rather conspicuous on the battlefield. His scars attest to that."

James then looked the sleeping man over, the sergeant's words giving him pause.

Clearly, he had been a soldier at one time; and if not, then he'd led a life that was prone to frequent acts of violence. Most conspicuous of all was a vicious scar that ran between his left elbow and shoulder. It was so deep it gave the illusion that the skin was adhered to the bone. A number of other marks of previous battles scored the body, and besides the left arm, the other most prominent mark was a scar that ran front-to-back on the left side of his head, near the crown. Upon first glance, it almost looked like the hair was parted there.

"You still look vexed, sergeant," James noted, as Sergeant Donaldson sat behind his desk, his chin resting in his hand.

"Beg your pardon, sir, this whole thing just seems so surreal. O'Connor spoke with an NCO from the 95$^{th}$ who was riding into Poitiers. They was placed in ambuscade by their officers with the expressed intent of protecting the man who now lies wounded in the other room. He was being chased by a slew of armed bandits…yet, when did robbers work in such large groups? They was awfully brazen in their pursuit, almost desperate."

"Did they capture any of them alive?" the major asked.

Sergeant Donaldson shook his head. "No. Most were killed outright or died soon after. There was one who was badly injured, yet the bastard blew his own brains out before they could get any information from him. And, of course, there was the last one, O'Connor blasted his head off. Clearly, sir, as much as the Duke wants this man alive, there are certain powers that just as vehemently want him dead."

Two days later, Corporal Harvey found himself in charge of the checkpoint. With an NCO required to supervise at all times, and with Sergeant Donaldson in temporary command of the entire company, this meant incredibly long shifts for his two corporals.

"Bugger me, but I wish they'd send some replacements and let us do some damn promotions already," the corporal grumbled as he yawned and stretched his arms overhead.

"Would be nice to see a promotion or two come down, as well," Private Douglas Farrow muttered, as he leaned against the fence railing that ran up to the road.

"Learn how to read and write," Harvey remarked. "I keep telling you lot, if you want to earn the NCO's chevrons, literacy will ensure your quickest path up the career ladder."

"I've been working on it," Farrow replied. He then asked, "Think you'll get your sergeant stripes once they do authorize us to fill all the vacancies?"

"I hope so," the corporal said. "Donaldson had a lousy two months date-of-rank on me and, therefore, got Billings' stripes when he bought it at Quatre Bras. Bloody army has since held off on practically all promotions while they downsize and go through all the mass-discharges, now that peace has finally come to the world. With our bloody luck, there will be an excess number of NCOs retained, and they'll all swallow up any chance we have at moving up the ranks."

While the two grumbled, as soldiers are prone to do, a dozen men approached the inn on horseback. They were better dressed than the brigands who had been recently slain, yet their demeanour denoted an equally sinister status. All were armed, mostly with pistols, though two also carried carbines. They all wore brown shirts and black trousers, with black greatcoats wrapped around them. Farrow first noticed them, his eyes growing wide as he quickly patted the corporal on the shoulder.

"Inform the major," Harvey said quietly.

As Farrow walked as quickly as he was able, without looking conspicuous, the four other soldiers at the checkpoint stood with their muskets shouldered.

"Bonjour, messieurs," Corporal Harvey said, as he held up his hand.

The riders halted and slowly spread out into a line of two ranks. They were very composed, and their instinct to manoeuvre into any sort of formation told the corporal these men were not amateurs.

"What business have you, so heavily armed?"

"The *king's* business," the leader of the group spoke. "We are hunting a fugitive that's escaped from justice."

"Are you now?" Harvey asked. "Do you have a name for this fugitive?"

"Not your concern, *lobster back*," the man retorted. The term he used was a derogatory name for the redcoats, referring to both their scarlet uniforms, as well as the British army's continued use of flogging as a form of punishment. "Now stand aside like a good little soldier boy so we can inspect the premises. If he is not here, then we will be on our way."

"I'm afraid I can't let you do that," the corporal replied, maintaining his composure despite the arrogance of the riders, as well as the blatant affront. "You could be bloody horse thieves for all I know. And you're not in any sort of a uniform, either. You got orders telling us who you are?"

The lead rider snickered, showing his teeth. The fact that he appeared to have all of them, and they were neither black nor discoloured, was telling.

"My name is Javier Foss," he answered, "Deputy to the Minister of Police, Joseph Fouche, Duc d'Otrante. As for orders…" He drew his pistol in emphasis, as did all of his men.

The riders with carbines pulled them from their scabbards. The four British privates brought their muskets to bear, though Corporal Harvey continued to lean on his, not allowing himself to be intimidated.

"*These* are my orders," Foss sneered. "Shall I write them out for you?"

"*Hold, sir!*" Major Webster shouted, as he stepped from the inn and walked briskly towards the men, his face red with anger. "You dare draw weapons against his Britannic Majesty's soldiers?"

"This man claims to be Javier Foss of the Ministry of Police," Corporal Harvey explained. "Says they are after a fugitive."

"Are they now?" James' mind raced, as he realized who these men were and who they were after.

"This is not your concern, *major!*" Foss snarled. "Your soldiers are interfering with the king's ministers and, as such, aiding a fugitive of royal justice!"

"France is under occupation of the British Army," James replied, maintaining his composure. Though he had little doubt that the man called Foss was speaking the truth, he was not about to give up the man who Wellington himself had placed under their protection. He decided to use the same ploy the corporal had. "Very well, but I'll need to see orders before I can let such a mob pass under arms."

A dozen weapons were suddenly levelled at the major as Foss' temper boiled over.

"As I said, these are my orders! Now stand aside, *les goddams!*"

The insult raised the ire of the British soldiers; for much in the same way they used the ethnic slur of 'frogs' to describe the French, so did their old nemeses use a similar derision towards the English. Literally meaning 'The God Damns', its origins went back to the Fourteenth Century and referenced the frequent use of profanity by English soldiers.

The doors to the inn were suddenly thrown open, and at least fifteen redcoats, led by Sergeant Donaldson, sprinted out onto the road. They quickly formed a single line and raised their muskets to fire. At the same time, the three upper level windows facing the road were thrown open, a pair of soldiers now visible in each, their weapons aimed at the riders.

"Very foolish," James said, shaking his head. Given that he had faced down Napoleon's Imperial Guard at Waterloo, he was not about to be intimidated by a handful of Fouche's men, armed with pistols, even if they were all pointed right at him. "You come into my checkpoint under arms, with no written orders, and you dare to threaten the soldiers of King George. Shoot me if you wish, but know that if one hammer falls on those weapons, every last one of you will die. Those not killed outright by my soldiers will be hung. The Duke of Otrante can then explain to the Duke of Wellington why his men committed an act of war against Great Britain."

Foss was in a state of fury. Thinking there were only a few redcoats at the checkpoint and not an entire company, he had made a profound error. And, though they had been in haste to leave Paris, he realized he should have taken the time to get written orders signed by Fouche. If, as he suspected, Wellington was behind the botched execution, then surely his soldiers were now protecting the fugitive marshal. His perpetual aggression had been his downfall, and he simply hung his head in resignation.

"That's better," the major said, his arms folded across his chest. "All of you, drop your weapons, then off your horses." As the riders complied, with a clatter of pistols and carbines onto the road, James turned to Sergeant Donaldson. "Sergeant, arrest these men and have them taken to the gaol in Orleans."

"Sir!"

"Damn your eyes!" Foss spat as redcoats surrounded him and his men, while others took their horses. "I am Javier Foss, deputy to the Duc d'Otrante, and you are allowing a dangerous fugitive to escape."

"Hold, private," James said to one of the soldiers, who had started to bind Foss. "If this man is who he claims to be, then he can return for his men once he produces written orders from the proper authority."

He then stood face-to-face with the police deputy. "Next time I recommend you try a little tact and persuasion, rather than brute force," he said with a half grin. "Such brutish behaviour is unbecoming of a gentleman, especially one in service to your king. Rest assured, your men will not be harmed in any way. They will be waiting for you at the Orleans gaol, along with their weapons and horses."

With a glare that bore utter hatred, Foss retrieved his pistol, remounted his horse, and quickly rode back towards Paris.

"Sergeant Donaldson," the major said, over his shoulder.

"Sir?" the NCO asked, running up to his officer.

"Dispatch twenty men to take this lot to Orleans. I'm certain either the inn or the outlying barn has a wagon you can use."

"Yes, sir," Donaldson replied, saluting sharply.

"And sergeant."

"Sir?"

"Once you reach Orleans," James said, "have bags placed over their heads. I don't want to risk any of these men being recognized by possible friends amongst the gendarmes."

James found their charge sitting upright in bed. His complexion was still rather pale, though at least he was able to eat some soup Corporal O'Connor brought to him.

"I heard the commotion outside," Ney remarked.

James sat on the chair next to the bed and explained all that had transpired.

The marshal laughed, though quickly grabbed his side, as it brought a sharp pain to his injury. "That'll enrage Fouche to no end," he managed to say after catching his breath.

"Once word reaches Paris, they will most certainly send the king's representative to have those men freed," James explained. "I suspect they will also come here, as they now suspect we have something to hide from them."

"In other words, it is no longer safe for me here," Ney acknowledged. His face was still damp to the touch, and he was a long ways from recovery.

"My instructions from the Duke of Wellington were to protect you at all cost," the major emphasized. "However, I was also told to be as discreet as possible and not cause an international incident when we are mere months into the first real peace seen in a generation. I think today's little incident may have wrecked that."

"Discretion was lost when those sharpshooters killed my assailants on the road," Ney noted. "Not that I'm ungrateful."

"Those were simple brigands," James said in return. "At least that is how I will portray them in my official reports to his grace. Most likely they were thieves and robbers who were offered pardon instead of the hangman's noose, if they were to track you down and kill you."

"And why do you think King Louis so wants me dead?" It was a loaded question, and Ney was curious to know if this English officer suspected who he was.

James chose his next words very carefully. "Perhaps," he said, "the king views your continued existence as a threat to his."

"And why would I be a threat to him?"

There was a long pause before the major spoke again. He glanced over his shoulder at the closed door. Finally he answered, "Because, *officially,* your corpse lies buried in Paris, shot a dozen times through the heart."

"Then you know who I am," Ney sighed in resignation.

"I know that a band of highwaymen were shot to pieces by British soldiers," James replied. "And I know that an unnamed individual who they attempted to rob escaped under a hail of covering fire from the 95th Rifles. I also know that the Duc d'Otrante is after a 'fugitive', whose name his men refused to divulge."

"And they will not stop until I am either out of France or dead."

"Understand this," James said with emphasis. "Whatever the Duke's motives are behind his desire to save you are not for me to question." He took a deep breath and allowed a slight grin before continuing. "Officially, Michel Ney, Marshal of France, lies dead and buried. Meaning this conversation never happened, and King Louis' hired mercenaries are chasing shadows."

Michel smiled. James left him to finish his soup and walked downstairs, where he found Sergeant Donaldson having a few last words with some of his men.

"The lads found a wagon over by the old barn, sir," he said, after he dismissed the soldiers. "They'll hitch a couple of the bandits' horses to it while tethering the rest behind. I've placed Harvey in charge of the detail. They should reach Orleans in a day or so, provided that wagon doesn't fall apart on them."

"And I suspect it will be about three days before King Louis' men show up to gain their release," James noted.

"Meaning we have four days, at the most, before those bastards are back here looking for their friend," the sergeant surmised. He looked towards the stairs. "How is he?"

"I doubt that he's fit for travel," the major replied. "Although he has proven himself to be quite resilient. Most likely Fouche's men don't know he's been wounded and will assume, when they return, that he's already made his way out of France."

"All the same, we'd best not keep him here for long, sir."

"I'll be ready to travel by tomorrow." The marshal's voice startled the men.

They looked up the stairs to see Ney leaning against the hand rail. He was shirtless with the bandage still wrapped around his waist.

"Very good, sir," James replied. "My men will have your horse and kit ready to go by morning. Also, I will give you one of my undershirts. You can't very well go back out in public wearing blood-soaked rags."

Though his side ached terribly, and he was still very weak with no appetite, Michel made certain he ate the rather large breakfast that was brought to him in the hours before dawn. Like Major Webster assured him, he would need all of his strength.

"It's time to go, sir," Corporal O'Connor informed him, as he was finishing up his sausage and eggs.

Ney's stomach turned in knots, and he fought to keep the meal down. The marshal donned his overcoat with stabbing pain shooting through his side, as well as his scarf and top hat.

"I took the liberty of servicing your pistol," O'Connor added as he handed Ney his weapon back. "One of the lads polished and sharpened your sword, as well."

"I'm indebted to you," the marshal said as he tucked the pistol into his belt.

"Just doing me duty, sir," the corporal replied. "I don't know who you are or why the major thinks you're so important, and he's not obliged to divulge his reasons to us rankers."

They made their way outside, where the cold chill of the wet December morning made them both shiver. Clearly the Irish NCO was eager to get back inside, where a pot of hot coffee awaited him. He carried a lantern, and they made their way through the blackness to where Ney's horse was tethered. The only people they saw were a pair of bored redcoats on guard duty, who David suspected had been half asleep before the sound of their approach alerted them.

"Here we are, sir."

Ney placed his left foot into the stirrup, yet the pain in his side made him move to the other flank of his mount and use his right leg to lift himself on. Corporal O'Connor had thought to offer him a hand, but knew their mysterious charge needed to be able to mount and dismount his own horse or he'd be in serious trouble within a day.

Ney looked down, touched his hat, and rode off into the mist of the predawn. It was cloudy and the sky black, so he could only chance having his horse move at a slow trot. He kept low in the saddle, his addled mind, still feeling the effects of exhaustion and blood loss, conjuring up images of would-be assassins lurking in the darkness and behind every tree. As a gust of wind and mist blew into his face, he shook his head, his military mind berating himself for thinking such nonsense. And while the damp chill was certainly uncomfortable, he reminded himself that, at least, it was not the hellish winter he had faced in Russia!

"Two hundred miles," he said to himself, judging the distance to Rochefort. "Two hundred miles to freedom…"

# Chapter XXII: Fouche's Downfall

Orleans Gaol
16 December 1815

Mounted Gendarme

Fouche had not slept in days. Having been reappointed as Minister of Police by Talleyrand, a position he held back in 1799, his benefactor's resignation and replacement as prime minister by the ultra-royalist Duke of Richelieu had left his own position rather tenuous. Given his past history of questionable loyalties, it was astounding that Joseph Fouche had been named president of the ruling commission after the fall of Napoleon, with an appointment in the Bourbon king's cabinet.

His rather dark history could not be fully suppressed, for Fouche had voted in favour of Louis XVI's execution twenty-two years before. As such, he was viewed with contempt by many within the royalist inner circles. Given this rather profound blight on his character, he had worked diligently to prove his loyalty to the Bourbon kings. Though his confidant and benefactor, Talleyrand, had disapproved of Fouche's overzealous attempts at placating the royalists, to include pushing for the death sentence of his own friend,

Marshal Ney. That the 'great traitor's' execution had been botched was of extreme embarrassment to both King Louis and Richelieu, and as Minister of Police, they held Fouche responsible.

The perpetrators of the charade had escaped persecution, for neither king nor prime minister wished to risk Ney's faked execution being made public. If they had pressed for prosecution of either the officer commanding or the soldiers of the firing squad, they risked abject public embarrassment. And so, Fouche had been given one order, and that was to discretely put an end to Marshal Ney, once and for all.

Since dispatching Foss and his men, Fouche had been assailed by vexations. He had no doubt that the insufferable Wellington would try to keep Marshal Ney safe through the use of his witless soldiers. The police minister hoped that if any of them did recognize the marshal, they would shoot their former enemy on sight. But, that would also bring the added risk of his escape being made public.

The door to his study was suddenly thrown open as Foss barged in.

"You come at a late hour," Fouche said with a minor trace of irritation. "I take it your mission has been successful?"

"No, sir," the deputy said, his eyes filled with anger. "Wellington's soldiers stopped us outside of Orleans. They arrested my men and sent me back, stating that I could only return for them with written orders from the proper authority."

The words were damning to both of them, and Fouche flew into a rage.

*"Idiot!"* he snapped, slamming the palm of his hand onto the table. "How could you let yourselves be disarmed and arrested by a handful of damnable redcoats?" He then raised his hand, not allowing Foss to answer. He stood and stared out the window of his study for some time, his hands clasped behind his back.

"Give me written orders, and I will release our men," Foss pleaded. "And I promise I will pursue Ney to the ends of the earth if need be!"

"No," Fouche said, turning to face him once more. "I will do what I should have done in the first place, and that is see to this affair personally. Your aggression, while useful in the past, has led you to become careless. I will go to Orleans myself, but know this, if I fall because of this, then you will go down with me."

Ney's side still hurt from where the pistol shot had pierced his flesh, but he had been unable to linger any longer at the coaching inn. The three days he had spent bedridden had been too few to help his wound mend, yet he knew that the British would not be able to protect him for much longer. Major Webster may have detained the assassins for a short while, yet both men knew it was just a matter of time before he received orders to release the men. The truth was, he had no real reason to hold them any longer. If not for the explicit instructions he had received from Wellington himself, there was a strong possibility he would have allowed Foss to search the inn, handing the marshal over to them once discovered.

As he made his way to the sea, Michel avoided inns, as well as most towns and any other place with a large number of people wandering about. He had paid a farmer a few francs to allow him and his horse to sleep in the barn. As he tried to make himself comfortable in the scratchy hay, the smell of farm animals overpowering, he found himself wishing for the soft bed he had at the coaching inn. Even more so, he cursed that he had been shot, nearly bringing about a permanent end to his journey. Had those brigands not caught up to him, he could have been to Rochefort and on a ship by now!

"Every mission order falls apart, once first enemy contact is made," he consoled himself and allowed himself a few restless hours of sleep.

The fact that assailants were in close pursuit confirmed Ney's fears that King Louis had sent more than just a handful of men to finish him. It was still more than eighty miles to Rochefort; at least three days ride, given the condition of the roads following the recent rains. He could only hope the distance he'd already covered was enough of a lead on his pursuers.

Fouche arrived at the gaol, having ridden all night in frantic haste. In addition to the French gendarmes were several British soldiers, including a sergeant that appeared to be in charge.

"I have signed orders demanding the release of a group of men brought here a couple days ago," he said curtly, handing the letter to the sergeant. "They are agents of the king, wrongly imprisoned by your soldiers."

"Is that so?" the soldier replied. "And on whose authority would you have me release them?"

"Why the king's, damn you!" Fouche snapped, shoving the orders across the table. "Do you not recognize the seal of His Majesty's Minister of Police?"

"Not for me to recognize," the sergeant shrugged. The corner of his mouth turned up slightly.

Fouche knew this English soldier was toying with him. Whether he was stalling in order to be difficult, or if he had other motives, Fouche could not say. As the minister's face turned a shade of red to match the soldier's jacket, the sergeant let out a bored sigh. "Seems all in order. Wait here, sir, and I'll have them fetched for you."

Ten minutes passed before the agents were all escorted into the foyer. All looked sullen and dejected, especially at the sight of Fouche himself.

"Horses are stabled out back," the British sergeant explained. "Some of your lads from the gendarmes are bringing their weapons up from the vault."

Fouche said nothing, only continued to stare coldly at his men. He reckoned he would dismiss the lot of them for their failure, leaving them to beg for scraps in the gutter along with the rest of the peasant class.

"What would you have us do, sir?" one of the men asked, as they stepped out onto the street.

"Head for Rochefort," Fouche ordered, keeping his back towards them. "If you do not bring me the head of the fugitive, then don't bother returning to Paris."

Knowing there was nothing left to be done, the Minister of Police mounted his horse and began the long trek back to Paris. After all he had survived over the years, from the Revolution to the rise of Napoleon, decades of war and political strife, the fall of the French

Empire, the First Restoration, Napoleon's return, and now the Second Restoration, one man had completely undone him. It infuriated Fouche, for Michel Ney was neither politically astute nor did he possess nearly the level of cunning and intrigue that Fouche did. The Duc d'Otrante had been the ultimate survivor, and now he had to face the king and tell him of his most grievous failure.

Major Webster returned to his duties soon after the incident at the inn. He was greeted by Colonel Stewart upon reaching his headquarters. The commander of 3/Grenadier Guards was seated behind James' own desk, his perpetually aching leg propped up.

"Colonel, sir," James said, as he saluted and removed his shako.

Stewart was not smiling but looked rather stern. "I heard about the incident at the coaching inn checkpoint," he remarked. "His grace had directed that this mission be conducted with discretion. Arresting a dozen of the king's agents and nearly starting a brawl between them and your own men is hardly discreet."

"Apologies, sir," James replied. "But Marshal…the man we were charged with protecting had been shot by assassins and was recuperating within. The agents were demanding that they be allowed to search the inn, I refused, stating that they needed written orders proving who they were. That's when they grew indignant."

"The Duke gave me a pair of messages to pass on to you," the colonel said, appearing to not have heard his major. "He recommends that the next time he gives you such a mission, you try a little tact and persuasion, rather than immediate brute force."

"Yes, sir." James cringed at hearing his own words repeated back to him. "I should make a personal apology to his grace for my failure to adhere to his directives."

"Who said anything about failure?" Stewart asked, raising an eyebrow. "I asked him if he was displeased with you, to which he told me, 'the good major has already proven he can fight; the rest he is learning quickly enough'. The second message he wanted me to pass on is that he is personally grateful for the protection your men gave his charge. He also wished me to underscore that if you will add a touch of cunning and guile to your already admirable qualities, you will have a bright future with the Grenadier Guards."

"Thank you, sir."

Colonel Stewart soon left him, and James sat down behind his desk and let out a deep sigh. As always, his rapport with the Duke of Wellington was a confusing mess of contradictions. He came to realize it was all deliberate. The Duke had an unusual style of leadership, one that never allowed subordinates to get too close to him, while also keeping them ever guessing as to his disposition. It also kept him from every giving the perception of cronyism or favouritism. While such cold differential methodology was not a style of leadership that James could ever see himself adopting, he figured that for the man who defeated Napoleon, it was what was needed.

The king was in a foul temper as his attendants helped dress him. He settled on a long frock coat this morning and would don his formal robes just before breakfast. Normally he would not wear such cumbersome garbs while he dined; however, there was the matter with the Minister of Police that he needed to rectify, and so he elected to dress formally.

As he plodded along the long corridor from his bedroom, his walking cane echoing on the polished floor tiles, he thought he heard the sounds of weeping coming from the tiny chapel. Louis peered into the small room, which was just large enough for a small altar and prayer bench, and saw his niece kneeling with a bundle of documents clutched in her hands. Her hand covered her eyes, and her face was red from sorrow.

"Leave us," the king said to his attendants with a wave. "Tell Richelieu I will join him presently."

As his servants bowed and continued on their way, Louis lumbered into the small chapel and knelt on the bench next to his niece, using his cane for balance.

"My child," he said soothingly. "What is it that vexes you so grievously?"

"This," Marie said as she held up the pile of papers.

"What have you been reading?" the king asked as he took them from her.

"Something I should have done months ago," Madame Royale replied. She then clutched her rosary and kissed it before whispering, "Forgive me."

"I don't understand," Louis said as he scanned the pages. "These are all news articles and official reports on Marshal Ney. What is your continued interest in the dead traitor?"

"Was he really a traitor?" Marie asked, her tear-stained eyes now fixed on the crucifix upon the small altar. "I know he renewed his allegiance to Bonaparte after promising to return him to us in an iron cage, yet can he be faulted when the entire army went over to the emperor? Everything I have read about the man I thought was the most odious traitor of all speaks of nothing but his service and personal bravery. His loyalty was not to any one man, but to France."

The king found he could not speak as his niece's words had caught him completely off guard. Though there were those within the Chamber of Peers that were suddenly expressing regret over the sentence handed down to the marshal, Marie Therese, Duchesse d'Angouleme, was the last person he would have expected this from.

"Ney was no revolutionary," she continued. "He did not send my parents to the guillotine, nor was he responsible for the death of my dear brother. He was simply a soldier, the 'bravest of the brave' according to both friend and enemy. Every victory he won was for France, not Napoleon. To think the horrors he witness, the hardships faced in service to his nation, and that we should turn on him so vilely at the end…oh God, *what have I done?*"

Such reactions would become common among many, even the most hardened royalists, in the coming weeks. And while the levels of emotion and expressed regret would vary considerably, in the very least it would become consensus that post-Napoleonic France had become very reactionary; having lost for a time any sense of pragmatism or common decency and respect for her bravest soldiers.

And yet, in that moment it seemed to King Louis that his niece had lost control of her senses. It was no mere weakness brought on by a soft heart either, for the Duchesse d'Angouleme had endured more hardships and shown greater courage in the face of adversity than any member of the Bourbon family. His heart very briefly wanted to tell her that the marshal lived, yet this was quickly supressed by his more practical side. Ney's survival added to his own shame at being betrayed once more. If Madame Royale were to rejoice in the survival of the very man whose death she had so vehemently called for, such would add to the king's sense of treachery. Instead, he simply kissed her upon the forehead and left her to her grieving.

It took Louis another five minutes to make his way down the corridor to his private dining chamber. His face was flushed, and an attendant quickly wiped the sweat from his brow with a handkerchief. Another helped the king into his formal robes as he took his seat behind the table.

"The Duc d'Otrante is here to see you, sire," the chamberlain said with a bow as he entered the hall.

"He can wait," Louis replied. "Have the prime minister or Prince de Talleyrand arrived yet?"

"No sire," the chamberlain answered.

"Send them in immediately once they do. I must speak with them before dealing with Fouche."

King Louis XVIII

"You have failed us, Fouche," King Louis said sternly as he swallowed another heaping mouthful of his breakfast.

The Minister of Police had arrived at the palace shortly after dawn. Word of the failure of his agents had already reached the king and cabinet and, given the cold reception he'd received from the moment he arrived at the palace, Fouche knew this meeting boded ill.

"Sire, with respect, it was an impossible mission," the minister protested. "Ney had a sizeable lead on us before the pursuit even began. My men were also twice ambushed by Wellington's damned redcoats! You should have sent the army or at least the gendarmes after him..."

The king slammed his fist down on the table, disturbing the plates, knocking over a fruit bowl and upending his wine chalice. He seemed to not notice as the highly expensive vintage streamed along the table, some of it running onto his robes. "You *dare* tell me what I should have done?"

As servants rushed in to clean up the mess, the king was calm once more. His chair creaked under the strain of his weight, the back threatening to break as he leaned back, his fingers steepled across his chest. Fouche fumbled with his hands behind his back and looked down at the floor.

"Forgive me, sire." There was a long, uncomfortable pause while Louis continued to stare at him. Fouche suspected the king was getting some sort of amusement at his discomfort.

"The Great Traitor escaped death through treachery," the king said in a condescending tone, like one would to a misbehaving child. "I would have expected that a master of treachery, like yourself, would have been able to bring him to justice. As it is, the incompetence of your men is reflected directly upon you."

"And while the commanding officer was arrested," Richelieu added, "he cannot be formally charged without drawing attention to the fact that his majesty's own soldiers would betray me so grievously. Can you fathom the sheer embarrassment for both your king and France, should word of this faked execution ever be made public?"

It was a rhetorical question, and Fouche maintained his silence.

"Stealth and cunning were required to finish the sentence handed down by the Chamber of Peers," Louis continued. "Were the gendarmes, or worse the army, sent in pursuit, it would not be very subtle, now would it? That insufferably egomaniacal Wellington has already sought to make me the fool in this matter Thanks to your ineptitude, he has succeeded."

There was another long period of silence as the king commenced eating once more. As he had not been dismissed, Fouche could only stand and wait to hear Louis' judgment. He chanced a glance over at Richelieu, who stood stoically behind the king, his face hard.

After several minutes, he could no longer maintain his silence. "What would you have of me, your majesty?"

"I would have you leave and never show yourself in my presence ever again," the king replied through a mouthful of pungent fish and eggs.

"Your services to the king are no longer required," Richelieu spoke up. "You are hereby banished from the Kingdom of France; never again will your presence be welcome within our borders. Your former loyalties to the usurper, Bonaparte, are more than sufficient justification for this. The royalists remember well your betrayal of his majesty's brother, who you helped send to the guillotine."

"Please, that was more than twenty years ago..." Fouche tried to say.

"And should you decide to ever make mention of the affair regarding the Great Traitor," the Prime Minster interrupted, "let us just say that your successor as Minister of Police is far more competent in resolving his majesty's little problems."

Joseph Fouche, Duc d'Otrante, left Paris under the cover of night. Widowed three years previously, his only family consisted of his fourteen-year old son and twelve-year old daughter. Surprisingly, he was allowed to maintain his title, which would pass on to his son, Paul Athanase Fouche, five years later, when Joseph died in exile in Trieste, Italy.

# Chapter XXIII: In the Shadow of the Iron Duke

## London, England
## 13 June, 1846

Field Marshal Sir Arthur Wellesley, Duke of Wellington

The journey by train from Paris to Rouen had taken Alexander only a few hours. However, the second leg from Rouen to Caen had lasted four days, two of which consisted of waiting for a coach to hire. Merchant traffic by sea between northern France and southern England was quite frequent, so booking passage across the English Channel had been comparatively painless.

Alexander soon landed at Portsmouth Harbour. A most awe-inspiring sight greeted him. The HMS Victory, the flagship of Admiral Nelson at the Battle of Trafalgar, forty-one years before. First launched in 1765, the massive 104-gun first-rate ship of the line had seen nearly five decades of active service before it was finally retired in 1812. The largest warship Alexander had ever set eyes on was the venerable USS Constitution. Yet, even that impressive vessel had little over a third of the total firepower possessed by the Victory.

From Portsmouth Harbour, Alexander journeyed by train north to London. Contrasting with the royal turmoil in France, the British

Empire was enjoying relative peace and stability under Queen Victoria, who had ruled since the death of her uncle, King William IV, nine years ago. What conflicts that did arise, such as the Anglo-Sikh War, took part on battlefields in remote colonies and were fought with mercenaries and indigenous auxiliaries, as much as British redcoats.

While France and other European countries had been left scarred and near destitute following decades of Napoleons wars, the British Isles had remained unscathed. Britannia was the only nation that played a major role in those seemingly endless conflicts that never had its shores invaded by a foreign army. After the decisive naval victory of Admiral Nelson at Trafalgar in 1805, no foreign naval force could threaten British rule of the seas, thereby allowing for unparalleled colonization and imperial expansion during the ensuing decades.

For all its wealth and glory, the British Empire was not without its dark and rather filthy underside, as Alexander saw the closer he got to London. The *Industrial Revolution* between 1820 and 1840 had led to vast increases in industrial technology and vast growth to the British economy. However, it also meant an extremely hard life in the factories for much of the working class. While wages of workers had increased substantially, the quality of housing in the cities was squalid and downright filthy for the lower classes.

By contrast, there was also the rise of a middle class during this time; professionals such as doctors, lawyers, and other learned types who lived to a much higher standard of living. It surprised Alexander to see such vast differences within the social orders. At the top were the very wealthy who lived in mansions, complete with servants, with the poorest crammed into derelict housing projects rife with disease, and middle class professions somewhere in between.

As the train came to a stop at Paddington Station with a loud screech, a conductor opened the door, telling people to 'mind the gap' as they departed. Alexander elected to walk the two-and-a-half miles around the historic Hyde Park to his destination, rather than taking a carriage.

London was a sprawling metropolis. The streets were crowded, and Alexander felt like he would suffocate in the mass of humanity. Amidst the throngs of people, factories, and shops stood innumerable monuments to Britain's past and present. Among those the young man hoped to see was the awe-inspiring Nelson's Column; a 170-foot monument finished three years earlier in commemoration of Admiral Lord Horatio Nelson's victory over the French and Spanish fleets at Trafalgar. Word had it the 18-foot statue of Nelson, atop the enormous column, faced in the direction of the HMS Victory's final docking place.

    It was only by chance that Alexander arrived in early June, just prior to the twenty-eighth anniversary of the Battle of Waterloo. Though the aged Duke of Wellington spent most of his days at his estate at Stratfield Saye, south of Reading, the date of his most celebrated victory always brought him back to *Number One, London* for the annual Waterloo Banquet. Those senior officers still alive would be in attendance, along with Prince Albert, the consort to Queen Victoria.

    Apsley House was an impressive sight, positioned on the southeast corner of Hyde Park, along a busy thoroughfare. Nearby, at the entrance to Green Park, sat a rather impressive monument known as *The Green Park Arch* or *Wellington Arch*. An impressive arch with a pair of columns on each side, it had been recently topped with a large twenty-eight foot statue of the Duke of Wellington astride his horse.[1]

    The wrought iron gate leading to the house was open, with a short flight of stone steps going up to the main door. A footman opened the door, raising an eyebrow at the sight of the young man.

    "Can I help you, sir?" he asked aloofly.

    "I was told to deliver this message to the Duke," Alexander replied, presenting the sealed envelope.

    "Yes," the footman replied, his expression unchanged. "His grace will see to it in his own good time."

    "Forgive me," Alexander said, "but my instructions were to deliver it in person." It was essentially a lie, although one he could forgive himself for. He wanted to make certain a message of such importance that he'd had to spend months traveling by sea, carriage, and rail would be delivered to the right person, and not left with a disinterested lackey.

    "Very good, sir," the footman replied, ushering him into the foyer.

A large and rather ostentatious house for a man who had spent decades living the harsh life of a soldier on campaign, Alexander was overawed by the spectacle of décor. Dozens of paintings, worthy of the masters, lined the walls, with gigantic candle chandeliers hanging from each end of the hall. Through the open doors at the end of the foyer Alexander could see a large staircase. It was what was next to them that caught his interest. Curiosity got the best of him, and he slowly walked to the end of the foyer to get a better look. It was a very large statue, not of Wellington, but of his former nemesis, Napoleon Bonaparte. Standing more than eleven feet high, the former Emperor of the French was naked, aside from a strategically placed leaf, with a cloak over the raised left arm which held a long staff. In the right hand was an orb, atop stood Victoria, the Roman goddess of victory.

"Boney hated it, you know," a voice said behind him, startling Alexander.

He quickly turned to see an old man in a dark suit. Much older now than in any of the paintings Alexander had seen, the distinguishing facial features, not least of which the aquiline nose, made the Duke of Wellington unmistakeable. Though he now walked with a cane, he kept himself erect, his strong aura never diminishing.

"Now," the Duke continued, "I was told you have an important despatch for me, though I'll be damned if I know who you are or who your message is from."

"Yes, sir," Alexander said, handing the envelope to the Duke.

Wellington was known for his ever stoic demeanour, rarely allowing others the opportunity to as much as guess his inner feelings. And yet, Alexander was certain he had seen the Duke's face twitch slightly, his gaze fixed on the seal as if it were drawing back memories from another life.

"Thank you, that will be all," Wellington said, with a short nod. He then abruptly left the room, scarcely using his cane, his eyes fixed on the envelope.

"This way, sir," the footman said, ushering Alexander to the front door.

"That's it, then?" he asked, as he stepped out onto the high steps that led to the gate.

"His grace does not socialize with messengers and errand boys," the footman replied coolly. "And since he has not asked for your employer's name or address, you can expect that he has no intention of sending a reply. Good day, sir."

As Alexander stepped back onto the busy street, he felt a sense of both being overawed and underwhelmed due to having been, essentially, shunned by the Duke of Wellington.

*But then, what did I expect?* He thought to himself. *Did I really think the Duke would invite me to tea?*

He shrugged and figured he hadn't known what to expect. Ever since he was a boy in school he had been fascinated by the Napoleonic Wars, in no small part due to Peter Ney's influence. Though he reckoned he should feel privileged to have even met the man who defeated Napoleon almost three decades ago, he was somehow expecting more.

He spent the remainder of the day walking the busy streets of London. It was a very short walk from Apsley House to Buckingham Palace. An impressive sight, sadly he could not get as close as he would have liked. The gates were closed this day with armed soldiers standing guard. These men wore red frockcoats with white belts around the middle and black trousers. Perhaps most distinctive were the tall bearskin hats, similar to those worn by Napoleon's famed Imperial Guard. In fact, it had been due to their victory over the emperor's best troops at Waterloo that the Grenadier Guards had earned the right to wear the famous head covers. In 1831, this honour had been extended to the other regiments of Guards Division.

Though fascinated by the sights of London, Alexander found himself longing for the comfortable familiarity of home. As he sat on his bed in the coaching lodge that evening, he pondered the meaning of his journey. Madame Ney had been hospitable enough, though silent regarding the letter. The Duke of Wellington had been cold and aloof, although Alexander understood that was how he treated pretty much everyone not close to him. And while he had had his suspicions for years as to the identity of his former teacher, the manner with which both the Duke and Madame Ney had responded to his letters seemed to confirm what his heart already told him.

The Duke of Wellington, Later in Life

    Wellington had taken his supper alone that evening. But, he was usually alone most evenings. His wife, who he had never been close to, except perhaps at the very end of her life, had passed on in 1831. His oldest son, also named Arthur, was a brevet colonel on the unattached list who had previously served with the Rifle Brigade. His other son, Charles, was the Member of Parliament for South Hampshire. And yet, he had little to no feelings of affection for either of his sons. Secretly, both had been a disappointment to him, although he would often chastise himself for placing unrealistic expectations upon them. He did have a certain fondness for his grandchildren, all sired by Charles, though he rarely saw them. The Duke had even ceased in the taking of mistresses. While this could have been explained by his rather advanced age, his reputation for extreme virility led many to speculate that he was simply bored with the idea. He was ever in the public eye, having only recently retired from politics, was still Commander-in-Chief of the Forces, as well as Constable of the Tower of London, and never one to miss a ball or formal social function. And yet, at the end of the day, the Duke of Wellington was ultimately alone.

He sat in his private dining room, which was adorned with massive portraits of the European monarchs from the Napoleonic Era. Behind the duke was King George IV of Great Britain, while directly across from him was King Louis XVIII of France; a man who he bitterly despised, and who also owed the restoration of his kingship to Wellington. Also amongst the portraits were King Frederick William III of Prussia and Emperor Franz I of Austria. As resplendent as the room was, it sometimes felt like a tomb to Wellington, for every man whose portrait adorned the walls had passed on years before. It was almost macabre that the portrait of Emperor Franz was painted posthumously, with his death mask used as the model for the artist.

The Duke found he had little appetite this evening, forcing himself to at least drink some hot soup with a glass of claret. In the soft candlelight, his eyes were fixed on the wax seal of the letter the young American had delivered earlier that day. Many years had passed since he last laid eyes on the crest pressed into the red wax, yet there was no mistaking it. It belonged to a man who had officially been dead for over thirty years, and yet his lungs still breathed life. A flood of long suppressed memories flooded his conscience as he opened the envelope and read the contents of the letter within:

*My Dear Duke,*

*By the grace of God I see that we both still live, with most of our friends and enemies gone to wherever the Lord has seen fit to send their souls. My own time in this world grows short, and it is only now, at the end, that I can finally come to terms with my incomparable fate. The histories have long since recorded that I died on the streets of Paris, executed by my own soldiers. And yet my heart, which I ordered the soldiers to aim for, still beats, at least for a little while longer.*

*Many times you and I were mortal enemies on the battlefield. At Bussaco, Pombal, and Redinha in Spain, and later at Quatre Bras and Waterloo in Belgium, each of us would have surely killed the other, if given the chance. Strange then, that at this late hour my one time fiercest adversary is now the only man that I can truly call 'friend'. Mind you, Peter Stuart Ney has many friends and acquaintances; the Marshal of France, however, has only one.*

*As the years passed, I have known not whether to praise or curse you for having saved me. Every day has been torture, not being able to see my sons or hold my beloved wife again. I now realize that these feelings were purely selfish in nature, and that I should give thanks to both God and Wellington for the opportunity to affect the lives that I have here in America.*

*In short, I thank you for giving me the opportunity of life and have the honour to be ever your humble and obedient servant,*

*Ney*

Wellington quietly folded the letter and walked over to a fireplace, whose embers glowed softly in the dark. He closed his eyes and seared the memory of the words into his very soul before tossing the letter into the fireplace. It immediately caught fire in the red hot embers, the flames reflecting off the Duke's face in the brief moment before the words were forever lost to history. But then, the words were not meant for posterity.

As Wellington returned to his dining table, he poured himself another glass of claret, and while still standing, raised his glass defiantly towards the portrait of King Louis XVIII.

"To the bravest of the brave!" he said.

Endnote:

1 – The Wellington Arch was moved to its current location in 1883. The massive statue of the Duke created controversy, and was considered rather egomaniacal. When the arch was moved, the statue was relocated to a separate display in Aldershot. The current statue atop the arch, known as *The Quadriga*, was added in 1912.

# Chapter XXIV: On to Bordeaux!

Rochefort, France
16 December 1815

Port of Bordeaux

It had been an arduous few days as Ney made his way to Rochefort. His side continued to hurt, and he was still in a far more weakened state than he would like to admit. He knew he needed rest, along with plenty of food, of which he had had very little of either since leaving the British outpost. Once he was aboard ship he would allow himself to finally relax. Travel by sea had never bothered him, and a month on the ocean would be the perfect time for him to recuperate.

The sun had long since set, and he could almost smell the sea breeze a few miles away as he approached from the main highway to the northeast. The land was dotted by a few small farming communities. Corn was a staple in this region, though in December all the fields were barren. He knew of a commercial port near the edge of the city, along the river. This would be the first place he would attempt to gain passage out of France. Ironic, that here he was attempting to escape via the very place where Napoleon had been captured when blockaded in by the British Royal Navy. This time, at least, there were no enemy warships waiting in the harbour.

There was a public house, as well as a number of shops, near the edge of the town. As Ney dismounted, he started to tether his horse to a nearby post when a strong hand grabbed him from behind by the shoulder. He spun around, instinctively reaching for his concealed pistol, when he saw the face of the man who'd startled him. Though his features were at least partially concealed by his tricorn hat, plus the shadows of the alley, the marshal grinned as he recognized him.

"By God," he sighed in relief. "Colonel Lehmanowski!"

The man nodded, his broad grin gleaming in the faint light. "You're a hard man to catch, marshal."

"As are you, John-Jacob," Ney replied, placing a friendly hand the Polish officer's shoulder. "I heard about your escape; a feat worthy of legend."

The colonel gave a nonchalant shrug. "I simply slipped out of my makeshift prison that even a child could have escaped from," he replied. "It is your method of cheating death that will be legendary, provided anyone ever hears of it."

"Well, I have not completely escaped yet," the marshal noted. "I still need to get to the harbour and find transport out of this place."

"You won't find it here," Jacob replied, shaking his head.

"What are you talking about?" the marshal protested. "There is a commercial port not two miles from here!"

The colonel motioned for Ney to follow him into the alley. A pair of gendarmes walked past, one holding a lamp in front of him. They were very attentive, as if they were searching for something, or someone.

"It is not safe for you here," the colonel explained. "Fouche was not as daft as the brigands he sent after you. As soon as you escaped, he sent his agents to the port cities. The gendarmes are now searching for a certain 'person of interest' who matches your description. When they approached me, I thought I was a dead man, yet it was not I who they seek. They refused to give a name, but the description they gave matches you almost perfectly, albeit, they said you were a Prussian spy or something of that nature."

Ney chuckled at the description. "Well, my mother's surname was Grewelinger before she married my father," he observed. "I was born in the French enclave of the predominantly German-speaking portion of Lorraine. I suppose I am as much German as I am French, with a trace of Scottish according to my mother."

"That would explain your size," the colonel chuckled, looking up at him. Like most men, Lehmanowski stood a half-head shorter than Ney. "A curse, my friend, you were born to achieve such a conspicuous size with distinct features."

Ney gave a tired chuckle, removed his hat, and ran his fingers through his hair. "Mother used to tell me that the colour of my locks was due to her distant Scottish ancestry," he observed. He then asked, "If not Rochefort, where then shall we go?"

"Bordeaux," the colonel replied. "The size of the city alone will give us cover and anonymity. Fouche's men and the gendarmes cannot cover even a small portion of the harbour. Besides, I think his majesty's agents are convinced you will make for the nearest port, and so are converging here and La Rochelle. Come, I know a safe way out of the city and away from prying eyes."

The two men waited a few minutes until they were certain there were no more gendarmes lurking about. Jacob then led his horse out of the alley, while the marshal struggled aboard his own mount. His side still ached terribly, yet the stitching of the British surgeon appeared to be holding, and he had yet to see any signs of gross infection. Still, he knew it would be some time before he fully recovered from the loss of blood he'd suffered. This also made the cold of the December night chill him considerably, despite his thick greatcoat.

"At least it's not the cold of the Russian winter...or of the grave," he whispered as he exhaled, and watched his cold breath dance in the faint lamplight.

Jacob guided him along a dirt path that ran along the river. Overgrown with weeds, it was clearly almost never used. It was a clear, moonlit night; and while this added to the cold, it also allowed them to see with relative ease. The farm fields on either side of the river, with the broken stalks left from the harvest, left an eerie impression on them as they shuddered in the breeze.

"Here we are," the colonel said, as he suddenly stopped in the middle of the path and dismounted. The far side of the river was intersected by a canal that ran due south. "I hate to do this to you, sir, but we must cross here. The bridge to the east is being watched, as is the main road. At least this won't be like fording the rivers during the Russian winter." He gave a macabre chuckle at this last remark.

Jacob had served on Ney's staff during that ill-fated campaign, and he, too, remembered how the brutal cold of the Russian winter had killed far more French soldiers than the Tsar's army. Napoleon had always been quick to remind both friend and foe alike that he had resoundingly defeated the Russian military, and it was the weather alone that had bested him.

As both men stripped out of their clothing, which they would tie to their horses' back in an attempt to keep it somewhat dry, Lehmanowski noted the freshly-stitched gash on Ney's side.

"By God, sir, when did you come by that nasty wound?"

"A few days ago," the marshal replied. "Can you believe it was a British surgeon who retrieved the shot and stitched me up?"

"That explains your delay," Jacob noted. "I confess, for a while I thought you had fallen to Fouche's assassins."

The two men stepped gingerly through the weeds and tall grass before guiding their horses down the rather steep embankment. Their naked feet sank into the cold, saturated earth as they slowly started to splash into the river. To the outside observer they would have appeared rather comical, as the only clothing they continued to wear was their hats.

The water was much lower this time of year and, thankfully, maintained its mild temperature. Ney quietly noted as he waded into the waters that now reached past his chest, it was not nearly as brutal as the liquid ice of the Russian rivers. He did feel a distinct bite of sharp cold on his wound, and he gritted his teeth as they swam their mounts across. The current was relatively slow and gave them little difficulty. Within ten minutes they stood shivering on the far side, their horses shaking themselves off, spraying their riders. Ney saw that while his undershirt and trousers had remained mostly dry, his greatcoat was completely soaked.

As soon as the men dressed as much as they were able, they remounted their horses and continued on their way. They continued to follow the canal path south for ten miles. The occasional farm house or shed lay across a short expanse of field, but for the most part it was completely deserted. The only sound besides their horses' occasional grunts were the gentle flow of the canal and the rustle of corn stalks from the harvested fields in the breeze. The path soon joined with a dirt road that angled to the southeast, away from a nearby village. They had begun their journey with nearly a hundred miles to go before they reached Bordeaux, and when morning finally came they had covered nearly half that. They soon took refuge in an old abandoned barn and managed to sleep a few hours. Ney hung his greatcoat in the sun, hoping it would dry before they moved on.

Surprisingly, there were no further incidents during the additional two days of travel before they reached the outskirts of Bordeaux. Famous for its wine, first introduced by the Romans in the 1st Century A.D., the climate was far more agreeable and decidedly warmer than Paris had been.

"Good God, man, you need a wash and a shave," Jacob laughed, as he looked a Ney's rather frightful appearance brought on by several days of scruff and sleeping on the ground.

"Perhaps my rough appearance will help conceal us more," the marshal chuckled.

Feeling the relative safety brought on by so many denizens gathered in one city, they rode boldly into Bordeaux. Though there were the occasional gendarmes mixed in with the populace, they seemed to pay the men no mind. The crowds had literally given them perfect concealment. They soon found an inn near the harbour, and while Lehmanowski went out to see about their accommodations, Ney took his first hot bath in at least two weeks. As he gazed into the mirror, he realized, between the days of scruff and his filthy appearance, he did not even look like the same man. Still, as much as it may have disguised him, he found it undignified and, therefore, resolved himself to shave before taking his bath.

He felt reinvigorated as he pulled himself from the tub, as he did so a sharp pain shot through his side. As he placed his left hand over the wound, he looked down at the gruesome scar on his upper arm.

"Yes, I've definitely had worse," he said quietly. As he finished dressing, the door was opened.

"Well, you do look like the Marshal of France once more," Jacob said, as he entered the suite, shaking his head. "I figured you would at least wait until we were underway before allowing your face to be shown again."

"It was uncomfortable," Ney replied. "I've never been partial to facial hair. I tried a moustache once. It was sparse at best, plus Aglae found it hideous." He immediately stopped and gazed down at the floor, taking in a deep breath and letting out a slow sigh.

Jacob forced a smile, though his expression conveyed that he understood his friend's pain. "You'll have to leave your name behind," he said, trying to change the subject. "Marshal Michel Ney is dead and must remain buried. We must forge a new identity for you." "And no change of name for you?" Michel asked.

"No need. The world all over knows of Michel Ney, Marshal of France. Who outside of our old veterans has ever even heard of John-Jacob Lehmanowski, Colonel of Polish Lancers? I'll bet most people cannot even pronounce my surname."

"Fair enough," Ney replied. "I'll not give up my surname, though."

"Seriously?" the colonel asked.

"It is not as if my family are the only ones to possess the name of Ney," Michel replied. "Forgive me, my friend, but I cannot find it in me to completely let go of my heritage."

"Alright, keep the name of Ney if you wish," Lehmanowski relented. "But you must drop your given name."

"Hmm," Ney thought for a moment. "Well, my father's name is Pierre. I could go with something along those lines."

"Your father?" Jacob asked. "You speak of him in the present tense. Is he still alive?"

"He is," the marshal acknowledged. "The old boy is nearing eighty, but he's still in decent health. We've rarely spoken over the past twenty years, although, I imagine that hearing his once-famous son was shot as a traitor will still be a great blow to his spirit."

"Well, sadly that can't be helped," the colonel stated. "Still, 'Pierre Ney' might be too conspicuous. How about Peter?"

"You think I should take the English pronunciation of my father's name?" Ney asked, raising an eyebrow.

"Why not?" Jacob shrugged. "Any thoughts on a middle name?"

"Strangely enough, I was never given one by my parents," Ney remarked. "Some men, particularly the nobility, have three or four middle names, yet I was born with none. My mother sometimes mentioned being of both Scottish and Germanic ancestry. I believe she said she was related to the Stuarts on her mother's side."

"Well, there you have it then," the colonel said. He extended his hand, "A pleasure to meet you, Mister Peter Stuart Ney."

"And to you, sir," Ney replied with a laugh, clasping Jacob's hand. "Now, did you get the writing material like I asked?"

"I did," the colonel answered. "Can't imagine why, though. I mean, who do you have to send letters to?"

"Two people," Michel replied. "Nothing that will give us away; just a single line to my wife, letting her know I live."

"Death was just the beginning," Jacob said, as he read over Michel's shoulder. "What the devil does that mean?"

"Something the Duke of Wellington said to me," the marshal stated. "It was also something that was said to Aglae. She'll also recognize the handwriting. I'll add, *'Love from America'*. How's that?"

"Completely clichéd," Jacob said with a chuckle. "Still, it will be total gibberish to any who might intercept it. At least Madame Ney will know that the king's agents did not get to you. Who's the other letter to? Surely not to Wellington!"

"No," the marshal said, shaking his head. "This goes to one other, who more recently saved my life."

John-Jacob had arranged for passage aboard a ship carrying wine to Philadelphia. It was set to depart with the early morning tide, out through the Bay of Biscay, across the endless miles of the Atlantic Ocean, and finally to the New World.

"You don't get seasick, I hope," Jacob chuckled, as they led their horses along the dock towards the ship.

"Never have," Ney replied, "although I've never been out at sea for this long."

"And just so you know, I put those two gold coins I asked you for to some good use," Jacob explained. "They bought us not only space for our horses, but got us each our own private cabins. There are about a dozen other passengers headed for America; a few were upset that I outbid them for the cabin space."

As they reached the ship, they saw a customs agent reviewing some paperwork with the captain. The other passengers were waiting impatiently on the dock for them to finish. The boatswain spotted the two men and walked over to them, his expression one of great enthusiasm.

"Ah, Mister Lehmanowski!" he said boisterously, clasping his hand. "You and your friend are free to board anytime. Leave your horses with my mate, and he'll make sure they're properly stowed. We made some space for them on the portside and arranged for sufficient fodder."

"Much obliged to you," Jacob replied, touching his hat.

The two men walked up the gangplank, much to the chagrin of the other impatient passengers. The customs agent glanced up at them. Both Jacob and Michel smiled and nodded. Even though he had looked the marshal square in the face, he paid him no mind and immediately went back to reviewing the manifest with the captain.

The sea air filled Ney's lungs as closed his eyes and breathed in deeply through his nose. He then leaned against the rail and turned back, gazing at the busy port. "Shall I ever see her again, Jacob?"

"You mean France?" his friend questioned in turn.

"That," Ney nodded, "but more importantly, Aglae. Will I ever see my beautiful wife again; feel the comfort of her embrace and the lovingness of her touch?"

"Only God can answer that," the colonel replied, grateful for a moment that he was a bachelor.

The marshal's expression was a profound amalgam of both relief at being alive and free, tempered harshly with the loss of being officially 'dead' to his wife and sons.

The customs agent finished his stack of paperwork and promptly departed to make his way over to the next vessel seeking to leave the harbour. The boatswain's whistle blew and, in a frenzy of activity, the ship made ready to cast off. Ney scanned the distant horizon as the wind blew large waves across the ocean, gusts filling the unfurled sails as the ship lurched forward. Despite the knowledge that it would be at least a month before they arrived in Philadelphia, he strained his eyes, almost as if he could catch a glimpse of what lay beyond. He never looked back.

James arrived at his detachment headquarters early that morning. Lance Corporal Farrow was filling in as his aide that week and was seated behind the desk in the outer office. Though there still had not been any orders allowing for NCO vacancies to be filled just yet, about a dozen new recruits had arrived at Major Webster's detachment. He had, therefore, decided to authorize a handful of appointments to what had previously been called *Chosen Man*. While technically still privates, soldiers with specialty skills or leadership potential were sometimes given the added pay, as well as allowed to wear either an arm band or single chevron. Soon after the wars ended, the army decided to make the position more permanent. While still an appointment rather than an actual rank, lance corporals were given the added pay and were usually aids to the full corporals. Douglas Farrow was especially proud of the single chevron he now wore on the upper arm of his tunic.

After their little 'adventure' a couple weeks ago, James found himself settled back into the tedium of routine. As a major, he found that the vast majority of his daily duties were administrative in nature. Technically, four of the company commanders within the battalion reported to him, with him and the other battalion major answering in turn to Colonel Stewart.

He was also quick to learn that with the wars over, his political savvy was far more important to his career advancement than his prowess at leading men into battle. He was still quite young and knew he was a number of years away from even being considered for lieutenant colonel. Still, from a purely 'political' standpoint, he was in a decent position. Colonel Stewart respected him, especially after his performance as acting-battalion commander at Waterloo. Their brigade commander, Major General Maitland, also thought well of him, having fought in the same action. And then there was the Duke of Wellington himself. Though their rapport appeared rather mixed and somewhat distant, James knew, even from afar, the Duke would be watching his career with measured interest.

A knock at his office door snapped him out of his reminiscing.
"Come!" he said.
"Beg your pardon, sir," Lance Corporal Farrow said, as he opened the door. "There's a messenger here to see you."
"Messenger?" James asked. "Who is he?"
"No idea, sir. He's a bloody frog is all I know. Doesn't speak a word of English, and I'm sorry to say I haven't picked up the local tongue just yet."

James shook his head and sighed, as he rose from his desk and followed his aide out into the foyer.

"Major Webster?" the man asked, his accent quite thick.

James rightly suspected, like Farrow said, that he probably did not speak English.

"Oui," he replied. The man then handed him a small envelope, sealed in wax.

"Qui est-ce du?" James said, asking who the message was from.

"Un ami, c'est tout ce qu'il me disait," the messenger replied, stating that it was from 'a friend', and that's all he was told.

James then nodded to the man, who promptly left the office.

He turned the envelope over in his hands. It was inscribed:

*Major James Henry Webster, Grenadier Guards*
*Army of Occupation, Poitiers*

"Who do you think it's from, sir?" Farrow asked, looking over his shoulder.

Most officers would have berated him for standing too close and not minding his own business, though Major Webster had a slightly more relaxed demeanour with his men, especially those whose extreme valour he could recall in vivid detail.

"I have no idea," he replied. He opened the seal and read the very short message. His face broke into a grin, and he let out a sigh of relief.

*The cargo you secured has safely departed for America. – N.*

# Chapter XXV: Relics of a Life Long-Lived

Cleveland, North Carolina
October, 1846
\*\*\*

Alexander found himself spending more time in Britain than originally intended. It was mid-July before he'd been able to set sail for America, and even then his ship had stopped off in Barbados, where sail repairs delayed their traveling onward until towards the end of September. It was mid-October by the time they docked in Philadelphia, and the young man was wondering if he'd ever get home. He'd been away for eight months, and his friend had been in poor health when he left. Would he still be with them by the time Alexander returned home or had he departed this world?

A storm had just unleashed its fury upon the township of Cleveland, North Carolina when Alexander returned. Winds howled and blew the rain into his face as he opened the wrought iron gate leading to the small manor house. Though it was only early evening, it was already dark, as was typical in the late fall. The glow of a lamp from the study window was all Alexander had to see by, and he kept the satchel with the cherished documents tucked under his arm as he leaned into the rain and walked quickly to the front step, giving a rapid knock on the door. A minute passed, and if not for the lamp light coming from the study, he would have surmised that no one was home. At length, the door creaked open. It was not the black footman who answered, but Peter Ney himself.

"Alexander!" the old man said excitedly, beckoning him in. The door closed behind him, and the howl of wind and a burst of rain against the door accenting his entrance.

"Good to see you, Peter," the young man replied, removing his hat. "I wasn't sure if you'd left us for good while I was away, but I am glad to see your health improved."

"The last winter almost took me," Peter replied. "And though I feel much improved, I have been left in a drastically weakened state. I am glad you've returned, for I sometimes wonder if I've seen my last summer."

"I brought a number of documents for you," Alexander said, pulling several thick envelopes from the satchel.

Peter grinned as he thumbed through some of the pages that were bound together with twine.

"It's been many years," he said quietly. He then looked to Alexander. "I deposited the rest of your retainer fee into your account. Should you decide to move to Boston, you can purchase a very nice house and still have plenty left to live on until you find employment."

"You are too generous, my friend," Alexander replied.

"Not at all," the old schoolteacher replied. "It is you who has been generous, completing such a long and arduous errand to placate the whims of an old man."

"It was truly an honour," Alexander emphasised.

Peter's servant soon entered, bearing a tray with a pot of tea and a pair of cups.

"Nothing stronger for you?" the young man asked.

"Not anymore," Peter replied. "Excessive drink has led to one-too-many unfortunate incidents over the course of my life. The weather is absolutely dreadful this night, please allow me to put you up in one of the spare bedrooms. I'll ask Jonathan to make sure there are fresh sheets and blankets."

"Thank you," Alexander said. "I would be grateful to not have to wander home in the pouring rain."

"Pneumonia almost finished me," the old teacher replied. "Can't let it strike you down."

The two men talked well into the night, with Peter asking pointed questions about the people and places Alexander had visited. He had been most curious about Madame Ney and was glad to hear she was still in good health.

"And beautiful still?" Peter asked.

"She was clearly the woman in the portrait," Alexander replied, bringing a smile to the old man's face. His journey had exhausted him, and Alexander soon excused himself.

The rain beat down on the roof, with the occasional crashing of thunder, until the late hours.

The sun shone brightly through the eastern-facing window the next morning. Alexander opened the shades and saw that while all was soaked from the night before, the glow of the sun offered a sharp contrast to the hellish storms. He dressed and made his way downstairs, where he found Peter in his study. Bundles of papers, brought back from France, were scattered around on various tables. Alexander wondered if the old man had even bothered going to bed the night before.

"Good morning, sir," Alexander said, though Peter appeared to not hear him.

The young man then noted an old parchment in Peter's handwriting. On it were a list of names, French officers from the Napoleonic Wars.

"The Marshals of France," Peter explained. "Napoleon created twenty-six *Marshals of the Empire*. Those you see listed are those created at the very beginning, in 1804. Of the fourteen official and four honorary marshals, only Nicolas Soult still lives."

"A good man is he?" Alexander asked.

"A good friend," Peter emphasised, "and a brave soldier. He led the decisive attack on the enemy centre during the emperor's greatest victory at Austerlitz. As for the rest…" He paused as he ran his finger down the list.

The young man noticed that Peter's shaking had become much worse, and he struggled to keep his finger still.

"They say Berthier committed suicide in 1815," Peter said, as he read through the names. "Personally, I think he was murdered by those damned Bourbons. Murat was arrested and executed by the King of Naples. Massena died of unknown causes in 1817, just two years after he became like Judas."

Alexander wanted to ask Peter the meaning of this last remark, but the old man abruptly continued.

"Brave Lannes died from his terrible injuries suffered at the Battle of Aspern-Essling. And Bessières, who was such a dear friend, was killed while conducting a reconnaissance mission in 1813 near Poserna-Rippach. Damn it all, but he was one of the best of us!"

Alexander wondered if by 'us' Peter was referencing all soldiers of the French Empire or was he, in fact, referring to himself as a marshal?

The young man soon had to say goodbye to his friend. Within a week he was headed north to Boston, though he promised Peter he would return, should the old soldier and schoolteacher have need of him. Peter promised then, when Alexander returned, he would finally answer that question which had lingered in his mind for years. It would not be a very long wait.

On 15 November, the old schoolteacher lay on his bed, eyes closed, and his breath coming in short rasps. A few friends, along with a doctor, were on hand, knowing that his time was growing short. Among them was the old Polish colonel, John-Jacob Lehmanowski. Unfortunately, the letter to Doctor EMC Neyman was late in arriving at his home in Indiana, and so he would be delayed in coming to Cleveland.

"Your friends are with you, sir," Alexander said quietly, clasping his old teacher's hand.

Peter still had his eyes shut, and he was muttering incoherently. A few intelligible words passed his lips. "Bessières has fallen," he muttered, referring to a Marshal of France named Jean-Baptiste Bessières, who commanded the cavalry of the old guard and had been killed by a cannonball on 1 May 1813. He continued, "The old guard is defeated...now let me die in peace." "Peter, please," Alexander said, clasping his hand even harder. "There is one last thing we must know, the question that you promised to give the answer too...*who are you?*"

The old man opened his eyes, which were now full of life and understanding. He looked up and smiled, squeezing his friend and former pupil's hand.

"I will not die with a lie upon my lips," he said, summoning the last of his strength. He then gave a content smile, and in his last words he repeated those words once said to the Imperial Guard at Waterloo.

"You know me...I am Ney, Marshal of France."

# Afterword

**Peter Stuart Ney** was buried in a mausoleum at the cemetery of Third Creek Presbyterian Church in Cleveland, North Carolina. Interestingly, the 'Stuart' name is misspelled as 'Stewart' on the tomb marker. Despite the claims and evidence supporting his assertion as being Marshal Michel Ney, the epitaph is rather ambiguous, stating he was a soldier of Napoleon, but giving no further details.

Grave of Peter Stuart Ney

Peter Ney's grave marker

Of Marshal Ney's family:

**Aglae Ney** died in Paris on 1 July 1854 at the age of seventy-two. Little is known about the remainder of her life after Ney's execution, only that she never remarried.

**Joseph Napoleon Ney** was allowed to inherit his father's title, *Prince de la Moskowa*. He died on 25 July 1857 at the age of fifty-four. As he died without male issue, the title of Prince de la Moskowa passed on to his youngest brother, Edgar.

**Michel Louis Felix Ney** inherited the title Duc d'Elchingen and continued to serve in the French army. He was killed at Gallipoli, during the Crimean War, on 14 July 1854, just two weeks after his mother passed away. The title, Duc d'Elchingen, passed on through his line, ending when his descendant, Michel Georges Napoleon Ney, died without male issue in 1969.

**Edgar Napoleon Henry Ney** was recognized as *Prince de la Moskowa* in 1857, after the death of his brother, Joseph. He married, though died without issue, with the title Prince de la Moskowa passing on to his brother, Michel's, line. It also came to an end with the death of Michel Georges Napoleon Ney in 1969.

The fate of Ney's third son, **Eugene Michel Ney**, is disputed. On the one hand, he is recorded as having died on 25 October 1845 at the age of thirty-nine, unmarried and without issue, though no other details are given. There was also the story of Doctor EMC Neyman, who claimed to be Eugene Ney and was sometimes listed in census reports as 'Eugene Neyman'. After Peter Ney's death, he came to Cleveland to 'claim the body of his father'. Doctor Neyman died in 1909 at nearly one hundred and one years of age. While Peter Ney's friends were ambiguous when placing the epitaph on his grave, the friends and family of Doctor Neyman proclaimed proudly that he was the son of Marshal Ney. Though it would be possible to prove or disprove these claims by DNA testing a descendant of Neyman against one of Marshal Ney's known relations, this has never been broached by either family.

Grave of Dr EMC Neyman

Of Marshal Ney's peers and associates:

**King Louis XVIII** remained on the throne of France, despite his many weaknesses and general dislike by the public. The Treaty of Paris, which formally ended the Napoleonic Wars, took a hard line against France, with borders retracted to their extent of 1790. Already impoverished after years of warfare, France was required to pay for the Duke of Wellington's Army of Occupation, at a cost of 150 million francs per year, over the next five years. An additional indemnity of 700 million francs was levied as well, in order to compensate Britain and the allies for their losses during the wars. Surprisingly, Louis attempted to maintain a more centrist, rather than ultra-royalist, government during the remainder of his reign. As Louis was childless, his wife having died while they were in exile in 1810, his younger brother, the Count of Artois, became his heir.

Due to his morbid obesity, Louis suffered from gout and gangrene in both the legs and spine. He died on 16 September 1824 at the age of sixty-eight, and was succeeded by his brother, who ruled as Charles X. Interestingly, he is the only French monarch of the 19th century to die while still ruling. Louis' fears that his brother's ultra-royalist tendencies would alienate the general public proved well-founded, as Charles was forced to abdicate following the July Revolution of 1830.

**Marie Therese, Duchesse d'Angoulême** became *Madame la Dauphine* upon the death of Louis XVIII, when her husband, Louis Antoine, became the heir apparent of King Charles X. Upon his abdication, following the July Revolution of 1830, Marie Therese ended up in exile once more, along with her husband and uncle. Spending the first three years in Britain, they later moved to Austria, where they were the guests of Marie's cousin, Emperor Francis I. She died of pneumonia 19 October 1851 at the age of seventy-two, just three days after the fifty-eighth anniversary of the execution of her mother, Queen Marie Antoinette. She is buried with her husband and uncle, Charles X, at the Franciscan Monastery church of Castagnavizza, on the border of Italy and Slovenia.

**Paul-Jean Poret de Morvan** survived the Battle of Waterloo, despite his battalions of the Imperial Guard being shot to pieces and suffering 60% casualties. He was imprisoned following the Bourbon restoration, though was released under a general amnesty in 1817 and later allowed to return to duty. In 1829 he was named Inspector-General of Infantry. He died in 1834 at the age of fifty-six. His name is among those inscribed under the *Arc de Triomphe* in Paris.

**Andre Massena** was disciplined by the royalists in order to prove his loyalty, though he retained his command of Marseilles. He died of an unknown illness in 1817 at the age of fifty-eight. He is buried at Père Lachaise Cemetery in Paris. He shares his tomb with his son-in-law, General Charles Reille, who died in 1860 at the age of eighty-four.

**Rémi Joseph Isidore Exelmans** lived in self-imposed exile in Nassau until 1819, when he was recalled to France. In 1828 he was named Inspector-General of Cavalry. Following the July Revolution of 1830, King Louis-Philippe awarded him the *Grand Cross of the Légion d'honneur*, and reinstated him as a Peer of France. He was further raised to Marshal of France in 1851, the year prior to his death. He died after falling from his horse in 1852 at the age of seventy-six.

**John Jacob Lehmanowski**, the former colonel of Polish lancers who had served on both Marshal Ney's staff, as well as Napoleon's personal guard, remained in the United States. He first settled in New York, later becoming a school teacher in Philadelphia. Around 1835 he moved to Indiana and purchased a farm. He was twice married, having seven children with his first wife before she passed away. In 1832 he published a short military history on Napoleon, and in 1836 he became a Lutheran minister. He spent much of the next twenty years traveling while giving both sermons and lectures on his wartime experiences.

Following Peter Stuart Ney's death in 1846, Lehmanowski was among those who asserted that Peter was in fact the famous Marshal of France. He died in 1858 in Sellersburg, Indiana, at the age of eighty-five. He was buried on land he had deeded for a cemetery; however, no markers remain.

# Author's Final Thoughts

The faked execution of Marshal Ney has been a legend among Napoleonic enthusiasts since 1815. While it sounds like a fanciful story on the surface, it has never been altogether dismissed. This is due to the preponderance of evidence that supports the theory that Peter Stuart Ney was, in fact, Michel Ney, Marshal of France. Granted, it is almost all circumstantial, the exception being the analysis of their respective handwritings, done in 1890 and again in the 1930s, which concluded that they were written by the same hand. A substantial portion of my research was found in James Augustus Weston's *Historical Doubts as to the Execution of Marshal Ney*. I was fortunate enough to find a copy through a company called Forgotten Books. A more detailed analysis of the evidence, as well as my own interpretations thereof, can be found on my blogsite: http://legionarybooks.blogspot.com/

# Further Reading / Bibliography

Weston, James Augustus. *Historical Doubts as to the Execution of Marshal Ney.* London: Forgotten Books, 2012.

Napoleonic Society on Marshal Ney:
http://www.napoleonicsociety.com/english/neya.htm

Davidson College official page on Peter Stuart Ney:
http://sites.davidson.edu/archives/encyclopedia/peter-stuart-ney

# Illustration Credits

Front Cover: *Marshal Michel Ney, duc d'Elchingen, prince de la Moskova*, by François Gérard, 1805

Chapter II: *Napoleon Reviews the Imperial Guard*, artist unknown

Chapter IV: *Charles Maurice de Talleyrand*, by François Gérard, 1809

Chapter V: *Les fils du Maréchal Ney*, by Marie-Éléonore Godefroid, 1810

Chapter V: *Joseph Fouche, Duc d'Otrante*, artist unknown

Chapter VII: *Marie Therese, Duchesse d'Angouleme*, Heinrich Füger, 1796

Chapter IX: *Aglae Louise Auguié*, artist unknown

Chapter XI: *Sir Robert Thomas Wilson*, by William Ward, 1819

Chapter XIX: Close-cropped image of *The British Defence*, by Chris Collingwood, licensed through The Waterloo Collection

Chapter XXIII: *Sir Arthur Wellesley, Duke of Wellington*, by Sir Thomas Lawrence, 1814. Licensed for use through English Heritage

*Note: All images are either licensed though applicable copyright holders, or else are in public domain*

# James Mace's previous Napoleonic works:

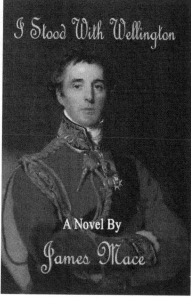

Find all of James Mace's books on his author's page on Amazon and Amazon U.K.

Official Website: www.legionarybooks.net
Facebook: http://www.facebook.com/legionarybooks
Blog: http://legionarybooks.blogspot.com/
Twitter: https://twitter.com/LegionaryBooks

Made in the USA
Middletown, DE
17 December 2016